Easy and Effectiv Development

M000267206

Given the current economic climate and budget constraints facing schools, funding for professional development is continually reduced. And yet administrators still need to find methods to implement new instructional initiatives, such as the Common Core State Standards. This important book provides leaders with a high quality professional development approach at a low cost—the Peer Observation Process. Outlined in manageable steps, this strategy will help leaders implement any new school initiative or instructional method, no matter the context.

This book will help you:

- Support staff with job-embedded learning that includes reflection and feedback
- Get your staff excited and engage them in ongoing collaboration
- Create teams and organize schedules
- Initiate and deliver tough conversations
- Address accountability and measure success

Based on an established and successful program, this book outlines an effective approach that is easy to implement and will help schools increase student achievement, strengthen school culture, and improve job satisfaction.

Catherine Beck leads a dual language International Baccalaureate elementary school in Summit County, Colorado, and is an adjunct professor at Concordia University.

Paul D'Elia is the co-founder of Shelf Leadership, LLC, an organization dedicated to expanding leadership education opportunities for high school students.

Michael Lamond is teaching language arts at a turnaround middle school in Denver, Colorado.

Easy and Effective Professional Development

The Power of Peer Observation to Improve Teaching

Catherine Beck, Ed.D.
Paul D'Elia
Michael Lamond

Routledge
Taylor & Francis Group

NEW YORK AND LONDON

First published 2015
by Routledge
711 Third Avenue, New York, NY 10017

and by Routledge
2 Park Square, Milton Park, Abingdon, Oxon OX14 4RN

Routledge is an imprint of the Taylor & Francis Group, an informa business

© 2015 Taylor & Francis

The right of Catherine Beck, Paul D'Elia, and Michael Lamond to be identified as authors of this work has been asserted by them in accordance with sections 77 and 78 of the Copyright, Designs and Patents Act 1988.

Library of Congress Cataloging-in-Publication Data

Beck, Catherine.
 Easy and effective professional development : the power of peer observation to improve teaching / by Catherine Beck, Paul D'Elia, Michael W. Lamond.
 pages cm
 Includes bibliographical references and index.
 1. Observation (Educational method) 2. Teachers—In-service training. I. D'Elia, Paul. II. Lamond, Michael W. III. Title.
 LB1731.6.B43 2014
 371.102—dc23
 2014007061

ISBN: 978-1-138-02390-1 (hbk)
ISBN: 978-1-138-02391-8 (pbk)
ISBN: 978-1-315-77620-0 (ebk)

Typeset in Optima
by Apex CoVantage, LLC

Printed and bound in the United States of America by Publishers Graphics, LLC on sustainably sourced paper.

Contents

Foreword

I am honored to provide this full-throated endorsement of *Easy and Effective Professional Development: The Power of Peer Observation to Improve Teaching*, in which Catherine Beck, Paul D'Elia, and Michael Lamond provide educators with a clear road map for improving student achievement via a pragmatic teacher professional development process that reliably improves teaching. I've had the privilege of working in the field of pre-service and inservice teacher development for over 30 years. During my career I have become acutely aware of the fact that most teachers receive virtually no meaningful instructional feedback regarding the effects of their teaching, or practical tactics and strategies for substantially improving their teaching. Instead, professional development consists of endless well-intended conferences, seminars, professional books and articles, webinars, additional college courses and the like—all of which obviously play an important role in developing one's knowledge base yet do not address the most essential element in human learning: actionable feedback. A teacher friend of mine summed it up well when he remarked, "I've been teaching high school math for nine years and student teaching aside, I've *never* observed a colleague teaching or received feedback from a colleague observing my instruction!" Research has confirmed that it is extremely difficult if not impossible to improve complex skill sets such as teaching, without ongoing meaningful feedback. One simple yet supremely powerful strategy to fundamentally change this situation is the Peer Observation Process (POP) delineated in this invaluable book. Structured peer feedback using the tactics described by Beck et al. is a brilliant example of what noted school change expert Michael Fullan calls "organized common sense." POP is cost effective, enhances collegiality, builds productive school culture and, most importantly, provides schools with a sustainable locally driven process for ensuring that each teacher in the building is developing his/her skills. I can speak from first-hand experience supporting schools in developing peer feedback programs as well as watching coauthor Mike Lamond leading the implementation of POP at his middle school in Colorado. Peer Observation is one important strategy for involving teachers in addressing the urgent need to ensure we are all involved in giving and receiving actionable feedback . . . or as I like to say, "Feedback—it *is* the breakfast of champions!"

Kevin Feldman, Ed.D.
Emeritus Director of Reading & Intervention,
Sonoma County Schools, Independent
Educational Consultant

Meet the Authors

Catherine Beck has been in education for the past 25 years. She spent the bulk of her career teaching before moving into administration positions including Director of Curriculum and Instruction followed by Principal.

Catherine currently leads a dual language International Baccalaureate elementary school in Summit County, Colorado. She just completed her doctorate in Instructional Leadership. Catherine is an adjunct professor at Concordia University in their online program. She mentors new Principals in Colorado through a Principal Leadership Program. The schools that she has led have won numerous state awards for growth in student academic achievement.

Paul D'Elia co-founded Shelf Leadership, LLC, to expand leadership education opportunities for high school students. Inspired by the work with Shelf, Paul transitioned to working with adults on various organizational development initiatives. For several years Paul was a faculty member for both Special Education and Social Studies at a rural high school in Colorado. During that time he served on the Building Leadership Team and District Instructional Leadership Team.

Currently, Paul is working in the Human Resource and Organizational Development field. Paul graduated from George Mason University in Fairfax, VA, with a degree in History and a certificate in Leadership Studies. He is a Myers Briggs Type Indicator (MBTI®) Certified Practitioner and Certified Relationship Awareness® Facilitator. Paul is an M.A. Candidate of Social-Organizational Psychology at Columbia University, New York, NY (2015 expected graduation). He lives in New York City with his wife and dog.

Michael Lamond has been teaching for over 14 years. His experiences range from inner city schools in Oakland, CA, to rural Alaskan villages. Most of his career has been spent at the secondary level, focusing on language arts instruction. At many of his stops, Michael has served on building and district leadership teams. Michael has also spent over 10 years coaching high school athletics, including boys' basketball and girls' soccer.

Currently, Michael is teaching language arts at a turnaround middle school in Denver, Colorado. He is serving on the building leadership team and has implemented a Peer Observation model at the school to provide support for staff and students.

Preface

The Peer Observation Process (POP) came about as a result of a district mandate requiring the Principal to be in every classroom every day. As a teacher leadership team, we knew that wouldn't be very effective, neither would it even be remotely possible. We were a struggling high school and we knew we needed to improve. Why couldn't the teachers be in each other's classrooms on a daily basis? Why couldn't the teachers be the ones serving as instructional coaches? We started to ask ourselves how we could utilize the expertise in the building to maximize the effectiveness seen in every classroom. After some tinkering, we were able to roll out the POP at the start of the school year. Where it was going to go, we had no idea. But, we were willing to experiment with it and see what we could get.

After several years of the POP being implemented at three different schools, we felt confident that *all* schools could see results from this process. District administrators and Principals can use this to mobilize their staffs towards a common set of school goals. The checklists provided will serve as a guide for how to focus the staff; it will give them the direction and the purpose, both so pivotal for staff buy-in. Teachers will see how this process serves as a completely non-evaluative way to receive feedback. The idea that they will only have feedback twice a year when they are formally observed is a thing of the past. They will become accustomed to giving and receiving constructive criticism, skills that are integral in the improvement cycle. Teachers will also appreciate the professional development pieces that are inherent in this process. Specific needs of EACH school become the focal points. It's no longer about hiring a "one-size-fits-all" consultant; it's about the individual school and the classroom and the students found therein.

The book is structured so that the reader can quickly justify why the process is beneficial and can use it as a concrete resource. It starts out with rationale behind the process. What becomes clear is that the POP is not just for struggling schools. *Any* school has room for improvement. *All* teachers want to get better. The following chapter explains the evidence supporting the concept of Peer Observations. There have been countless studies showing that when teachers observe other teachers and actually talk about pedagogy, the level of instruction grows. There are direct links connecting Peer Observation to higher test scores, higher teacher retention, higher staff morale. Not coincidentally, each school that is mentioned in the book has experienced all of these factors. The several chapters in this book address the finer points of setting up the program in individual schools. From identifying school leaders to creating the time, from making the groups to having the difficult conversations, we try to lay out all that could be encountered over the life of this process. There is then a link between the POP and the implementation of the Common Core. Many schools are having difficulties with the transition. With the POP in place, schools can expedite that process, ensuring that all teachers are prepared for the upcoming (or current in many cases) transition. Finally, we have included firsthand accounts from those who have participated in this process. They range from first-year teachers to 20-year veterans, from those in the classroom to those in charge. You will see how the process affects all who are involved.

We have also included several of the checklists that the schools have used. These are by no means the only ways to monitor. We wanted to show the progression, the changes of thought, the varying areas of focus. Again, each school will be able to tailor a document to fit its individual needs. We've also included a survey gauging the comfort level for teachers giving and receiving feedback, for their beliefs and expectations around peers observing peers, and for their expectations around the process in general.

What started as a conversation in the Principal's office around district mandates has blossomed into a process where schools utilizing it have seen tremendous growth and the accolades that go with it. The schools using it have realized that in order to truly succeed, *every* teacher should be a coach.

Introduction

With the huge financial cuts districts across the nation are facing, a practical solution for offering effective, professional development must be found for all school districts. Teacher instructional expertise is one of the most important variables affecting student achievement (Sparks, 2002). Darling-Hammond and McLaughlin (1995) suggested that teachers who know a lot about teaching and learning, and who work in an environment that allows them to know students well, are the critical elements for successful learning. Creating and implementing a successful professional development plan is paramount in today's era of accountability that demands results in student achievement. Possibly the only people that feel more stress than today's teachers would be the administrators.

No other factor more strongly influences student achievement than the classroom teacher (United States [U.S.] Department of Education, 2010). Teachers must have access to effective ongoing professional development if they are going to be successful in increasing student achievement in this day of accountability for educators. A comprehensive analysis of the nationally representative Schools and Survey Staffing Survey (Institute of Educational Sciences, n.d.) showed that the number of hours offered for sustained professional development for teachers, as defined by that which lasts for more than eight hours, has decreased since 2004 (Wei, Darling-Hammond, & Adamson, 2010). With the current economic climate, funding for professional development has been reduced. These budget cuts hinder the abilities to enhance classroom instructional practices through content-focused, job-embedded professional development, thus increasing the need to provide cost-effective, practical solutions.

"Not only is professional development an integral component of school improvement efforts, it is the single largest monetary investment in school reform" (Desimone, Smith, & Ueno, 2006, p. 181). In addition, given that school districts across the country are facing financial and budget deficits, it seems that making use of in-house experts to provide professional development would make sense. "Not only treating, but utilizing teachers within a school empowers them as leaders and produces transformational leadership within the context of the schools" (Desimone et al., 2006, p. 207). Teachers who receive substantial professional development, an average of 49 hours as studied by What Works Clearinghouse, can boost their students' achievement by about 21 percentile points (Yoon, Duncan, Lee, Scarloss, & Shapley, 2007). Peer Observation can offer up to 36 hours, or four hours a month of professional development per school year. Through the use of a Peer Observation Process, teachers can engage in ongoing collaborative discussions about instruction, thus providing for effective professional development centered in the context of their everyday jobs. "Given the centrality of teachers' professional development to school improvement efforts and the amount of money spent on it at the national, state, and local levels, increasing the understanding of how state, district, and school administrators can best provide and deliver professional development is a worthwhile endeavor" (Desimone et al., 2006, p. 180).

Administrators need to ask themselves the following questions:

- Is the present method of instruction getting me the results that I want? If so, how am I maintaining this in my building? How do I bring new staff members on board?

- If not, what changes am I going to make and how am I going to offer ongoing job-embedded support for my staff members to accelerate the learning curve of the new initiative?

This is the story of three very different schools that have implemented the Peer Observation Process (POP) to realize changes in instruction that have resulted in increases in student achievement and improvements in culture and morale. A rural high school, a rural dual language elementary International Baccalaureate school, and finally an urban middle school all used POP to observe and improve instructional practices used daily in the buildings. Each school had a different focus. This is the story of three faculties taking charge of their own professional development and driving the changes needed to move forward. The professional development offered in this process is ongoing and job embedded, situated in the very environment of their day-to-day duties. It cost nothing but time. It is an effective way to provide sustainability within the building. It is not dependent on a particular administrator as long as the subsequent administrators continue to provide the time needed to do the work.

You will see that the Peer Observation Process is not the answer. It is the process in which to find the answers.

Sound Basis for Peer Observation

We are a small rural school in the Colorado mountains with urban problems.

There was a desperate attempt to define the problems in the high school; the opening quotation is an example of an explanation often heard in the halls and community coffee shop. "With urban problems"—What did that mean? Was it a discipline issue? How about lack of resources? Perhaps. Probably. The issues were most likely similar to ones experienced nationwide ("urban problems" was not wrong, but too specific albeit edgy and attention grabbing). The school was focused on almost everything but solid, consistent instruction.

Quality Instruction

After a string of four Principals in as many years, a state audit of instruction was mandated. Morale and the local newspaper headlines were low. The steady stream of "failing school" rhetoric and spreadsheets of low state scores had ushered in the Comprehensive Appraisal for District Improvement (CADI) team to provide an in-depth, comprehensive look inside the school's classrooms. It was found and noted that the school had "pockets of good instruction." The report revealed what many knew and struggled to address, not because of competency, but because of the limits of the current professional development structure.

The school had had its fair share of consultants, speakers, and trainers come through the library on staff professional development days. Our school was just one piece of the documented historical cost of professional development in the state ($26 million as noted by the *Denver Post*). There were dynamite lessons taking place, effective grading practices, and engaging projects with real-world application; but not all the time and not in every classroom. The "pockets of good instruction" had to be opened and revealed through collaboration and increased professionalism of teachers. The Peer Observation Process was the answer as it was born organically and developed formally.

The Peer Observation Process at its core addresses the issue of providing consistent, quality instruction in every class, for every student, every day. That is how it began and that is what it achieved. Today, it is seen as something much bigger. It can spread any mission or initiative in a consistent and quality-driven manner. The Peer Observation Process (POP) does this because it recognizes some very significant realities. One, teachers benefit from and strive for increased professionalism. They each bring an expertise to the table. POP fuels this through empowerment and collaboration. Teachers love to be recognized for what they know, but they also acknowledge they do not know everything and that their peers are a great place to look for a balance of strengths. Second, Principals struggle to be present in classrooms on a consistent basis. The desktop calendar, if you can see it, or the iCal chime becomes irrelevant when a parent phone call comes through or a discipline action needs attention (and don't forget the printer cartridges need changing!). Many Principals strive to be instructional leaders, and many are (and are hired to be), but, unfortunately, the strategy of direct instructional coaching and feedback is a tough priority to fulfill for one person.

Culture

The Peer Observation Process sets up a culture of instructional coaching maintained not by one person, but by the entire faculty of experts—the teachers. Indeed, POP places "every teacher as a coach." The process is a vehicle for spreading the commonalities any building leader would like to see in each classroom. The star performers of a faculty open up their toolboxes of what is working. All faculty members have the opportunity to share key insights on lessons and classroom experiences. You will quickly see not only improved instruction but also a culture that nurtures continued development with little to no cost. There is no shortage of talent in education, despite what many critics with a national voice will have you believe. I would imagine you are reading this because you are an educator and you are now pausing at the idea of talent in education. Yes, you have stars in your building and in your district (you are one of them!); but you feel the policies (the voices of a strategy) coming out of the conference rooms are just not getting the spotlight in the right area. The Peer Observation Process as part of a professional development plan is more than a policy, it's a culture that finds, builds, and spreads talent. The policies (many of them very effective) need this culture, not the other way around.

"Change fatigue" is certainly not our language but is a great topic when it comes to talking about the importance of culture. Mission statements and shared values are effective tools to weather change. The Peer Observation Process culture offers continuous occurrences of staff members connecting their practices to the overall mission and objectives. Thoughtful and meaningful feedback defines and spreads shared values. Staff starts to feel less fatigued about what is changing and more energized about the possibilities of achievement. Leaders have an imbedded system to capture the strengths of top performers. The best part is the leader plays a supporting role in a process that is teacher—front-line staff—led. The Common Core State Standards (CCSS) are sending a wave of change across the nation's schools and policies cannot be relied on to react quickly enough or represent the true experiences of teachers. Use of a peer-driven culture clears the clutter, establishes what is important, and focuses on effective implementation.

The effective implementation we experienced at our high school in the mountains was seen through a series of snapshots. The obvious was seen through snapshots of quantitative measurement, positive scores, and upward movement of longitudinal student growth. The other view, perhaps less obvious but more powerful for future growth, was that of a typical Friday morning staff collaboration meeting. If you were able to see an actual visual representation of the evolution, through film or photography, of these morning collaboration sessions from before POP began to the start of its third year, you would witness the successful tale. Teachers were rarely late, they brought baked goods for everyone to share, and they seriously and studiously discussed student achievement and educational philosophy until the very last second before having to open their classroom for first period-waiting students. Morale was good. Headlines were good. Achievement was good.

Adapt to Change

At this moment discussion and planning was about forward progression. Yes, an initiative to reduce "pockets of good instruction" and spread great instructional practices is ongoing and requires time to build the comfort needed for deep, meaningful feedback. However, the process starts to build on top of itself. One strength of the Peer Observation Process is its ability to flex and react to current needs and objectives. Schools will find that the process can aid in implementing anything from making better use of technology for instruction to a massive curriculum overhaul.

New findings and knowledge enter the education sphere at lightning pace. A district or building leadership team cannot get policies written fast enough. Certainly, the Principals cannot do it all alone. The Peer Observation Process can diffuse knowledge faster than lunch lines fill on "Thanksgiving Dinner for Lunch" day. The Peer Observation Process will be instrumental for rolling out the effective use of the Common Core State Standards.

The National Association of Secondary School Principals (NASSP) has stated in its Common Core literature "the CCSS will radically change curricula, state assessments, school culture, and professional development." During a NASSP presentation about the CCSS, they highlighted key targets such as "the collective mindset of the staff is central to the ability to get things done" and "growth performance is the result of work, effort, and deliberate practice." The Peer Observation Process has those three elements at its core. Teachers embrace the work and effort it takes to retool a lesson after receiving feedback. An environment that respects deliberate practice energizes them. Because the observations are informative and supportive, rather than evaluative, practice is the common understanding. After all, aren't doctors "practicing medicine"? Teachers need a professional boost and can honorably practice their craft within a Peer Observation Process. In fact, many teachers gladly participated because it allowed an open forum in which to hone lessons that would eventually be evaluated by a supervisor.

NASSP has also noted that a key ingredient for CCSS implementation will be customization. Agreed, learning will be student driven, less confined to years, grades, and time, about accountability, and about higher order thinking. NASSP exclaims "customization demands collaboration!" The Peer Observation Process shares their list of what this means: "less hierarchical, less bureaucratic, less resistant, and more open to innovation." In fact, the process staff engages in during the observation and feedback sessions are precisely aligned with what the CCSS are asking students to do. A culture of higher order thinking based on collaboration and critical thinking can be developed in all corners of a school.

More "How"

The POP culture is going to give you high-caliber instructional practices. The Common Core State Standards have taken care of the "what" leaving the "how" as the important implementation step. As Vicki Halsey (2011) discusses in *Brilliance by Design*, we must make a shift that looks like this: "teachers dedicating 70 percent of their preparation to how (learning design) and 30 percent to what (content) they will teach." Halsey highlights that traditional preparation breakdowns look the opposite. The POP accomplishes an effort to increase the amount of time teachers are engaged in conversations about "how" they are getting the important information across. The collaboration among teacher groups will spread the most effective instructional practices throughout the building as observations take place and feedback is provided. This process creates a culture that supports only the best work being done and effectively decreases the amount of poor instructional practices. The whole thing is democratized and done from the bottom up. Supervisors end up observing a class for evaluation and seeing the teachers' best work that perhaps has been incubated over time through targeted feedback and mentoring.

There are concerns out there about the CCSS, such as "they are killing innovation" or are "too static in a dynamic world" (Washington Post Blog, The Answer Sheet, "8 Problems with the Common Core Standards"). The POP culture recognizes that the CCSS is not a curriculum, but standards that need a creative and collaborative environment to make them work as effective and relevant tools. Teachers use each other as resources to bring the standards alive and adapt them to local learning needs. Much of what is seen in a Peer Observation group is exactly what is expected in a CCSS influenced classroom. A common culture among teachers and students appears. The CCSS ask students to "persevere through problem solving." Teachers are doing the same as they respond to classroom needs with the help of peer feedback and suggestions. They do not rely on a policy to solve the issue (or restrain them from doing so); they collaborate with a possibility-driven mentality.

The POP also addresses change through moderation. As noted in Karen Golden-Biddle's (2012) *MIT Sloan Management Review* article, "How to Change an Organization without Blowing It Up", the most effective change is a balance between immediate large-scale change and small pilot programs. Within a Peer Observation group, moderate levels of change are introduced at a digestible rate. Instructional leaders can introduce practices by modeling and allow others to work on elements over time. Individuals have control over the rate of change as they lead the observation cycle with targeted areas of focus drawn from reflection and analysis.

Foundation and Growth

The evolution of the Peer Observation Process really grew as it took hold in another school with some similarities and enough differences to test the integrity of the process. The Peer Observation Process "moved down the hill" into an elementary school in the adjacent county and carried the professional development plan with it. The new staff was assured that they too would see results and that discomfort, at first, was to be expected. The process was now being mapped out formally and the luxury of retrospect contributed to the strengthening. The initial stages require a culture shift and that low comfort and trust levels are normal. Getting to the real hearty feedback sessions takes time. Here is a reflection from Kendra Carpenter, a teacher at the elementary school:

> When I first learned about Peer Observation I felt nervous. Having my peers in my classroom observing me was an intimidating thought. As we began the rotations I worried about my inevitable turn. What would people think? What would they say? As I observed my colleagues I realized how much I enjoyed having the opportunity to see what they were doing. As a student teacher, I did not appreciate the time we were given to observe in classrooms. With Peer Observation, not only was I learning from my colleagues, but it also afforded me the opportunity to reflect on my own practice. I was not judging them, but learning to respect what they did. Plus, I gained new ideas that I could integrate in to my own classroom and could offer some suggestions based on my own expertise.
>
> Two years later, I have grown to appreciate this process. I look forward to it. We have elevated the level of our teaching through Peer Observation. We have grown closer as professionals through Peer Observation. I now feel that I have a safe place to share my doubts about my teaching without penalty. I know that my team will come in and give me honest, yet kind, feedback. Through our

dialogue, I have brought parts of my teaching from my subconscious to a conscious level. I am aware of why I do what I do daily. I am able to hold a higher level professional conversation because I have taken the time to reflect on the research and my beliefs as a teacher. Even if it is not my turn to be observed I have a group of people in my building that I can turn to for help. They have been in my classroom and know my students so their feedback is helpful and meaningful. Now, I always have them with me as I teach. We are not individual classrooms functioning on our own, but rather a group of professionals supporting each other towards a common goal: success for all of our students.

Theoretical Framework

The stories and personal excitement over success are compelling and real. So, too, are the facts and theoretical framework. The theoretical framework for Peer Observation can be found in Vygotsky's (1978) theory of human development and the zone of proximal development. At the heart of Vygotsky's theory lies the framework that human cognition and learning is social and cultural rather than an individual phenomenon (Vygotsky, 1978):

> The teacher's zone of proximal development is thought of as a learning space between his or her present level of teaching knowledge consisting of content (theoretical) and pedagogical knowledge and his skills and his next (potential) level of knowledge to be attained with the support of others.
>
> (Eun, 2010, p. 2)

This implies that cognitive development, or acquiring higher mental functions, is possible only through the social interaction between a novice and a more capable person that ultimately leads to internalization by the individual (Eun, 2008). As discussed earlier, Principals can and do act as instructional leaders. However, solely looking to the Principal is not realistic and ineffective. The Peer Observation Process mobilizes the building leaders and star performers to support and coach new and struggling teachers. An environment of trust is established when even the star performer opens him/herself to feedback on a lesson. The novice finds a place to contribute meaningful insight by way of a stimulating and motivating workplace.

Vygotsky's theory is based on the notion of a more capable person supporting the development of a less competent person by mediating the less competent person's interactions with the environment. "By providing the symbolic mediators (i.e., knowledge and skills) and supporting their use, the less competent person becomes able to use them on his or her own" (Eun, 2010, p. 3). Thus, the interchange of ideas involving instructional strategies among the teachers involved in the Peer Observation Process may empower the less competent teacher and allows for multiple opportunities to practice and receive feedback within the context of the team.

Vygotsky emphasized the importance of goal-directed interactions needed to lead to the internalization and development for new ideas. Guskey (2000) described one type of professional development using observation techniques. This occurs when teachers observe each other and then convene to give feedback (Guskey, 2000). Guskey suggests that both the observed and the observer benefit greatly from this type of professional development. The observed teachers receive constructive feedback and the observer can learn from closely monitoring and evaluating the instruction in the context of his or her own instruction (Guskey, 2000). The process of observing another's teaching may provide valuable insights into aspects of one's own teaching practices (Guskey, 2000). Vygotsky's (1978) theory indicates that interactions between the expert and the novice benefit both participants.

Developing Comfort and Trust

Getting a Peer Observation Process off the ground and integrated into an existing professional development framework is relatively easy and requires almost no expense. At onset you can expect "J-Curve" development starting with forming groups and building trust and comfort and then quickly rising to instructional improvement. We will talk more in-depth about set-up and logistics further along in the book, but the sound basis for this process includes addressing some barriers. As Kendra tells us above, she felt "nervous" and initially a little "intimidated." This is natural and expected as getting over the idea that this process is informative, not evaluative, will be a very real barrier.

Many educator professionals have historically viewed the Peer Observation Process as evaluative in nature, thus producing a reluctance to embrace the process (Richards & Farrell, 2005). Straughter (2001) did an action research study to determine barriers to Peer Observation in a large urban school that housed grades kindergarten through 8th grade. Data were triangulated using observations, interviews, and surveys. The study lasted 18 months and the results revealed that there were barriers to overcome in order to implement a successful Peer Observation Process. Teachers reported psychological and social barriers, including vulnerability when receiving feedback, and difficulty critiquing a colleague (Straughter, 2001). Time away from students and student learning was also listed as a barrier, thus causing teachers to not want to leave their classrooms. Time and scheduling were the final barriers found as a result of the study (Straughter, 2001). Conclusions reached as a result of this study were that teachers need training to successfully implement a Peer Observation Process. Issues such as scheduling and time allowed for the actual observations needed to be a priority of the school dedicated to fully embracing a Peer Observation Process (Straughter, 2001).

Implementing POP will require some creative solutions to honor the time needed. Teachers will need regular (weekly or biweekly) time to meet in their peer teams. In addition, the observers will need class coverage or flexibility in using "prep" time. As we all know, class time and prep time are very sacred to staff. Leadership will be responsible for really communicating the value and mission of the process. Mentor teachers, instructional leaders, and overall respected personalities will have to be brought on board first to then build buy-in from the ground up.

In the beginning of our experimentation with the Peer Observation Process, our Principal would not even be present when the peer teams were meeting. It communicated trust. The integrity of the program relied on its being peer driven and non-evaluative. The leadership support was there to drive the importance and value. This was important as some teachers were defensive and routinely missed observation time and lightly engaged during feedback sessions. It only took a few cycles and key role models going first to be observed to put the process full steam ahead.

The Peer Observation Process can offer collaboration and collegiality, qualities highly valued for today's professional development models. Giving teachers the time and opportunity to learn from each other supports Vygotsky's (1986) theory of bidirectional learning, wherein both parties benefit or learn from each other. In this continuous cycle of observing and being observed lies the possibility for an improvement in student achievement, an increase in teacher self-efficacy, and the implementation of an effective, ongoing professional development model run within the context of a school building.

2 What Does the Research Say?

We have all spent countless hours in professional development workshops or conferences that felt like a complete waste of time. These "sit and get" models delivered by consultants who knew very little, if anything, about our school always provided an initial burst of enthusiasm that would eventually fade as the lack of follow-through became apparent. Teachers would head back to school energized with some new concept to try. Alone, they would implement the new initiative in their own little classes and eventually regress to their old teaching habits. There had to be a better way to change practices for teachers. What did the literature have to say about professional development and Peer Observation? How could we get these teachers to take charge of their own professional development to effectively make real changes to their everyday practices?

The use of Peer Observation as a form of professional development aligns with the adult learning theory that contends that adults learn best when they are actively involved in their learning and where past and present experiences are considered in the acquisition of further knowledge (Haslam & Seremet, 2001). According to Knowles (1984) the adult learning theory focuses on the need for adults to be involved in the ongoing planning, implementation, and evaluation of their learning (Knowles, 1984). Knowles challenged the pedagogical model of learning, where adult learners were passive recipients of knowledge and in turn, developed the andragogical model for learning (Knowles, 1980). This andragogical model is based on five assumptions, including that adults are viewed as self-directed learners and that adults are often the richest resources for one another. Adults become ready to learn "when they experience a need to know or do something in order to perform more effectively in some aspect of their lives" (Knowles, 1980, p. 11). Next, an adult's orientation to learning is life centered, and finally, "for the most part, adults do not learn for the sake of learning, they learn in order to be able to perform a task, solve a problem, or live in a more satisfying way" (Knowles, 1980, p. 12).

Adult Learning Theory

Investing in effective professional development is a commitment to both adult and student learning (Holloway, 2002). According to the adult learning theory when considering professional development, the following suggestions should be taken into consideration:

1 Adults will commit to learning when they believe that the objectives are realistic and important for their professional and personal needs. They need to see that what they learn through professional development is relevant and applicable to their day-to-day activities and problems.

2 Adults want to be the origin of their own learning and should therefore have some control over the what, who, how, when, and where of their learning as long as it meets the criterion of increasing teacher capacity to affect student achievement.

3 Adults will resist activities they see as an attack on their competence.

4 Professional development must be structured to provide support from peers and to reduce the fear of judgment.

5 Adult learners need direct, concrete experiences for applying what they have learned to their work.

6 Adult learners do not automatically transfer learning into their daily practices.

7 Coaching and other kinds of follow-up support are needed so that the learning is sustained.

8 Adults need to receive feedback on the results of their efforts. Professional development activities must include opportunities for individuals to practice more skills and receive structured, helpful feedback (Speck & Knipe, 2005, p. 73).

Fullan (1991) states that the ultimate purpose of professional development is to create individual and organizational habits and structures that make continuous learning a valued and endemic part of the culture of learning and teaching (Fullan & Steigelbauer, 1991). Consequently, professional development can be considered a "cornerstone of systemic reform efforts designed to increase teachers' capacity to teach to high standards" (Desimone, Porter, Garet, Yoon, & Birman, 2002, p. 16).

Professional Development Design

The design of many traditional professional development activities is based on the assumption that achievement can be gained through the vertical transmission of ideas from experts (Park, Oliver, Johnson, Graham, & Oppong, 2007; Sparks & Hirsh, 1997). This approach to professional development views teachers as relatively passive recipients of researchers' knowledge and the trainer's expertise (Lieberman, 1995; Sparks & Hirsh, 1997). This top-down approach is largely ineffective because it is driven by a deficit view of teachers that is reactive and remedial in nature (Baron, 2008). The focus for these expert-driven trainings tends to be on what is being taught rather than what is being learned by the teachers (Strucchelli, 2009). Professional development activities in the past have often ignored the critical importance of the job-embedded context in which teachers work (Lieberman, 1995). The outdated inservice model of professional development does not address the issues of teacher isolation or the promotion of inquiry-based learning and collegial relations among staff members (Bowers, 1999).

Current research trends suggest using models that promote more collaborative, contextualized, and skills-based learning while focusing on the teachers as the learners (Speck & Knipe, 2005). Whereas traditional forms of professional development focused on the end result, such as a particular teaching strategy, process-focused professional development has a much broader focus and encourages ongoing skill development among teachers (Strucchelli, 2009). This style of professional development tends to build internal capacity and sustainability. "With an emphasis on internal capacity, the leadership of professional development efforts comes from the faculty itself, and a large part of the professional education takes place in the classroom with the teachers engaged in authentic teaching" (Reeves, 2009, p. 75).

Characteristics of High-quality Professional Development

In researching high-quality professional development, there are several qualities that consistently emerge. These qualities include a focus on content and how students learn content, in-depth, active learning opportunities, links to high standards, opportunities for teachers to engage in leadership roles, extended duration, and the collective participation of teachers from the same school, grade, or department (Desimone et al., 2002). High-quality professional learning is intensive and sustained. It is directly relevant to the needs of the teachers and students, and it provides opportunities for application, practice, reflection, and reinforcement (Reeves, 2010). Peer Observation seemed to deliver on all of these requirements.

Several studies have found that the intensity and duration of professional development is related to the degree of teacher change (Shields, Marsh, & Adelman, 1998). According to Hiebert, Gallimore, and Stigler (2008):

> Research on teacher learning shows that fruitful opportunities to learn new teaching methods share several core features: (a) ongoing (measured in years) collaboration of teachers for purposes of planning with (b) the explicit goal of improving students' achievement of clear learning goals, (c) anchored by attention to students' thinking, the curriculum, and pedagogy, with (d) access to alternative ideas and methods and opportunities to observe these in action and to reflect on the reasons for their effectiveness.
>
> (p. 15)

Follow-up training, opportunities to apply and practice, and coaching are essential components necessary to effect changes in teacher performance after the initial introduction of a new theory or instructional strategy. In this context, professional development becomes an ongoing rather than an episodic process (Burke, 2000).

While the ultimate goal of all professional development is to help increase student achievement, educators can classify professional development goals into two subcategories: professional growth goals and student-centered goals. Results-based professional development is more effective when the teachers work in teams to achieve a common goal determined by the team (Burke, 2000). The goals should drive the teacher's self-discovery, be measurable, and be attainable.

Three structural components are paramount for a successful professional development program. These components include offering sufficient time for practice, activities, and content necessary for increasing teachers' pedagogy and fostering meaningful changes in their classroom practices (Loucks-Horsley, Hewson, Love, & Stiles, 1998). By allowing opportunities to take place during the school day, reform types of professional development are learned and practiced in a real-life teaching environment:

> Opportunities for active learning may include the opportunity to observe expert teachers and to be observed teaching; to plan how new curriculum materials and new teaching methods will be used in the classroom; to review student work in topic areas being covered; to lead discussions and engage in written work.
> (Garet, Porter, Desimone, Birman, & Yoon, 2001, p. 927)

Finally, ongoing discussion and effective communication skills among teachers regarding content and instructional strategies fostered through regular collaborative meetings bring a sense of professional support for those involved in the process. Collaborative discussion among teachers who confront similar issues can facilitate change by encouraging the sharing of solutions to problems, as well as by reinforcing the sense that with time, improvement and change is possible (Garet et al., 2001).

Benefits of POP and Professional Development

A considerable amount of literature on peer coaching and observation suggests that the professional development of teachers can be improved through experimentation, observation, reflection, the exchange of ideas, and shared problem solving (Bowers, 1999; Buchanan & Khamis, 1999; Pressick-Kilborn & Riele, 2008; Zwart, Wubbels, Bergen, & Bolhuis, 2007). Peer Observation empowers teachers by giving them control of their own learning, offering opportunities for dialogue, and improving collegial interactions (Bowers, 1999). "The most profound professional development comes from teachers observing each other's lessons, doing a play-by-play analysis, and sharing ways that the instruction could be even tighter the next time" (Kenny, 2010, para. 5). Bullough and Pinnegar (2001) suggest that teachers and professionals negotiate their understandings of practice through reflections and learning conversations. Peer Observation recognizes the value of prior knowledge and experience by providing teachers with the opportunity to reflect on their experience as well as the opportunity to have that knowledge and experience affirmed (Gordon, 2004).

Self-study of teacher education, or Peer Observation, is more likely to contribute to effective teacher educator professional development than accountability measures from the outside (Schuck, Aubusson, & Buchanan, 2008). Self-study provides a means for teacher educators to reflect on their teaching practices and consider ways of enhancing student learning and achievement (Loughran, 2002). This process has a strong reflective component, but also involves supportive discussions with colleagues. Through the act of observing and discussing, both parties in the Peer Observation, or self-study, learn and reframe their practices (Schuck et al., 2008). Observing other teachers teach is beneficial to both the observed and the observer (Ingersoll & Smith, 2003). One of the greatest benefits attributed to Peer Observation is the mutual appropriation, or bidirectional learning experienced by both the observer and the observee (Ash & Levitt, 2003; Mento & Giampetro-Meyer, 2000; Vacilotto & Cummings, 2007). "The person being observed benefits from the feedback which is focused and context specific while the observer refines an ability to define and identify attributes that promote a quality experience for students" (Martin & Double, 1998, p. 168).

Teachers in Charge

With teachers in charge, professional development is teacher sponsored and teacher driven, and they become responsible for determining, developing, and refining their own teaching practices (Dantonio, 2001). Cooperation is promoted among the staff members enabling them to improve their instruction in ways that develop naturally within the context of their daily teaching (Howley & Howley, 2004).

Peer Observation serves as a vehicle for fostering collegiality and collaboration within a building. Fullan (1991) argues that the power for change lies in teacher collaboration. Collaboration among teachers leads to many benefits. One of the benefits is an increase in student achievement and improvement of instruction (Schmoker, 1996). Collaboration can be seen as essential for learning. Working in isolation limits one's learning capacity (Fullan, 1993). Collaboration and collegiality can help develop teacher leaders and bolster teaching professionalism, which begins with the premise that the knowledge must be thoughtfully shared (Lemlech, 1995). Collegial discussions assist teachers in making the tacit explicit and are vital for the development of knowledge, skills, and expertise in practice (Loughran, 2002). Loughran (2002) also goes on to suggest that having "teachers working together, collaborating and teaming in ways that provide professional support for one another leads to improvements in practice as the sharing with, and learning from one another offers meaningful ways of framing and reframing existing practices" (p. 57). Vygotsky's (1986) theory contends that all learning takes place through social interaction with peers. Using a collegial and collaborative structure for faculties reduces teacher turnover, which tends to be high in rural communities. There is a clear link between positive teacher perceptions and student achievement in rural schools. Such positive perceptions must be connected to social, professional, and emotional relationships among teachers in schools (Hughes, 1999).

Relationship building and collegiality among staff members must be a priority if schools hope to retain teachers, especially in rural and remote schools (Jarzabkowski, 2003). The common culture of isolation in rural schools has major implications for the effective use of collaborative professional development. The collaborative problem solving in the inquiry process has been shown to break down teacher isolation and collectively empower teachers (Elliott, 2004). In order for collaborative, job-embedded, professional development activities to be effective, schools must first recognize and address this aspect of the school culture that opposes such collaborative learning (Strucchelli, 2009).

Peer Observation occurs when teachers are observed by other teachers; it is a collegial experience, not an evaluative one. Constructive feedback is given and the goal is to offer professional support. Critical conversations among staff members provide a means to generate thinking about pedagogy embedded in teaching and learning episodes (Loughran, 1997). When the reflective feedback is given collaboratively, the understanding of educational practices is enhanced for all involved (Bowers, 1999).

For Peer Observation to be successful, it must be carried out in an environment that is nonjudgmental and one in which learning and improvement of those involved is the primary focus (Richards & Farrell, 2005). Teachers who participate in regular reflective dialogues with others become more reflective about their own practices. Because reflection leads to learning, it is a necessary step in professional growth and improvement of daily practice (Hertzog, 1995). When properly implemented, peer feedback practices allow a teacher to learn from two perspectives: learning from one's own experience through self-reflection, and learning from a peer's classroom experience through the constructive feedback (Wilkins, Shin, & Ainsworth, 2009). This pedagogical approach fosters professional dialogue, encourages self-assessment, and facilitates seeing one's own practices through a different perspective.

The Three Stages of POP

Peer Observation should occur in three stages (Hammersley-Fletcher & Orsmond, 2004). The first stage is the pre-observation meeting in which specific areas are targeted for improvement, while the second stage is the actual observation (Strucchelli, 2009). Finally, the third stage involves the constructive feedback given in a collaborative model (Hudson, Miller, Salzberg, & Morgan, 1994). The observation alone is not enough: observations must be supported by critical reflection of the classroom practice given through shared critical reflection (Peel, 2005).

In Whitney Point, New York, a form of Peer Observation was utilized with a format called "teacher rounds." A lead teacher and a coteacher planned a lesson utilizing an identified instructional strategy (City, Elmore, Fiarman, & Teitel, 2009). A team of teachers would then come in to observe the lesson. Immediately after the lesson, the team of teachers that included the ones presenting and the ones observing would sit together to critique, discuss, and reflect (City et al., 2009). This format was viewed as successful in terms of improving instructional strategies and also for providing hands-on, professional development for all staff. Teachers also felt that it was positive in that it focused on student learning and came from their own staff members whom they deemed credible (City et al., 2009).

Peer Observation is a practical and invaluable means of professional development for any district (Bourne-Hayes, 2010; Cosh, 1998). Teacher observations that serve as vehicles for professional growth, rather than performance evaluations, can benefit everyone involved from administrators to the teachers themselves. Schmoker (1999) states, "If we consistently analyze what we do and adjust to get better, we will improve" (p. 56).

More and more teachers and administrators alike are viewing this kind of professional development as collaborative in nature. This kind of professional development can serve as a practical and relevant source for student improvement for all schools struggling in today's volatile financial crisis (Harmon, 2001). Situating professional learning inside the school day may also encourage the participation of less-active teachers, who may not normally participate in activities held outside the school or after school hours (Showers & Joyce, 1996). Through this method of professional development, teachers feel empowered, as they are viewed not only as the professionals, but also as the local experts providing in-house constructive feedback to their peers (Bowers, 1999).

Many teachers have a thirst for dialogue and would like opportunities for collaboration and discussion about successes and challenges within their classrooms. Collaboration is a construct that holds great potential for the study of school improvement (Chance & Segura, 2009). Implementing a Peer Observation model offers the opportunity to change the "closing the door to teach" culture in schools (Hansen, 2010, p. 52). A facilitated dialogue among peers, which traditionally has been between a supervisor and a teacher, now takes place routinely, offering a practical, ongoing form of professional learning (Buchanan & Khamis, 1999). This process is an effective way to take the best staff development projects and transform them into practice that teachers actually try and use in the classroom immediately (Hansen, 2010).

Through Peer Observation, teachers open their classrooms to their colleagues and begin to move beyond the isolation common to many schools of today. When teachers engage in inquiry into their own practice, the discussions that occur around the observations are grounded in the questions being addressed, and these discussions consequently promote focused professional dialogue that result in positive instructional changes (Strucchelli, 2009). Peer Observation goes beyond implementing an idea presented at a workshop and moves more towards a staff development that builds on collegiality, collaboration, self-discovery, and the solving of real problems of teaching and learning (Fullan, 1991).

The literature was supportive of the Peer Observation Process. It aligned perfectly with the adult learning theory and the need for collaboration. Gone were the days of teaching alone in isolated classrooms, using the same strategies that sometimes yielded success. The teachers' doors would be opened and their instruction would be examined by their peers. This process would work. It had to work. The stakes were too high for it not to.

3 Setting Up the Program

Armed with the research and knowledge supporting Peer Observation we set out to create the ideal process to transform our school. There were 23 teachers on our staff. Knowing that we needed to implement a new model for professional development we made some decisions. We divided the entire staff, paraprofessionals included, into four teams, each one led by an instructional leadership team member. We then had to agree on what first-best instruction looked like. The "Gradual Release of Responsibility Instructional Model" was chosen as the template for which all instruction would take place. A checklist was created that would be used in conjunction with the observations.

Our school was fortunate enough to have weekly collaborative time built in to the schedule. This time would be devoted to the Peer Observation feedback sessions. For schools that are not afforded this luxury, time could be utilized before or after school as well. We certainly have also met at these times throughout the school year in order to fit all of our meetings in when needed. It was decided that during a two-week cycle that one member of each team would be chosen as the teacher to be observed. All team members would take a planning period and go in unannounced to observe. Consequently, the teacher of focus would be observed eight different times during the two-week period. This would produce enough observations to prove to be an accurate picture of the instruction happening within the class. After the two weeks were up, the team would reconvene to process the observations and give feedback to the teacher.

Establishing Buy-In

Creating buy-in and a sense of comfort for the process would take some skill. We felt it was important that the introduction of the process come from the leadership team and not from administration. The instructional audit report, (CADI, as described in Chapter 1) was reviewed with the staff thus creating a sense of urgency for a solution. Certainly having an instructional audit helped to readily identify areas of need. Problems are difficult to repair if stakeholders do not have a clear understanding of exactly what they are. Team leaders met with their teams and then discreetly discussed each other's feelings about the process. Some teachers were unfazed by the idea. Others were not comfortable at all. To pave the way, each team leader volunteered to go first in the observation cycle. The process was now in motion.

We realized right away that there would need to be some time spent on creating a trusting environment. Everyone agreed that if all that ever happened was a pat on the back and an "atta boy" commentary given, then it would be a total waste of time. How did we move forward in having those critical conversations that resulted in actual change in practice?

The team leaders met with administration to problem solve the issue of giving feedback that was both constructive and corrective. They learned to lead the conversations by asking pointed questions. The checklist had a place for strengths observed and also a place entitled, "I wonder about." At the initial meeting, the teacher coming up to be observed would be asked for what he/she felt was his/her strength and also an area of need. This area of need would then be documented in the "look fors" by all of the observing teachers. In that sense, the path was set to give correctional feedback in response to a particular area of need.

Gauging Comfort Levels

Was every teacher thrilled with this process? Absolutely not, particularly at first. Teachers felt vulnerable having to open their doors to unannounced visitors. It is hard to expose a weakness, especially to one's peers. One teacher came to the office before her two-week cycle of observation and said, "It is one thing to be observed by my Principal. I expect that and am comfortable in that setting. It is another thing to be observed by my peers and I am a nervous wreck!" Gone were the days of teaching in isolation. This new culture of transparency was both frightening and energizing at the same time. As the months passed the conversations became richer. Trust was being built, and a sense of true collegiality and collaboration around instruction was apparent. In truth, it did take months to build the trust necessary for true transformation to take place. Teachers had to believe that the relationships were grounded enough to survive what their team members could possibly see as a critically constructive suggestion. Once the teams crossed this threshold, however, the magic started to happen.

The goal was support focused on improving instruction. The process was not evaluative in any way. Rarely did the team leaders speak to the Principal about another colleague. Never were names revealed. The beauty of this process was that the teachers in the building were driving their own professional development, based on their needs, in a job-embedded environment. The professional development was ongoing, providing sustainability within the building, completely separate from the administration. This requires trust from the administration in regards to the staff. Administrators have to be willing to let go of control of this process in order for it to work. Certainly if administrators have done an exemplary job in hiring then there is a veritable wealth of talent on every staff. If not, perhaps administrators need to review faculty placements and make some changes. Teachers are professionals and they are perfectly capable of not only managing, but also leading their own professional development.

Data From the First Survey

After one year, a survey was given to teachers to gauge their feelings about the process. The survey was divided into three sections. Section I focused on the teachers' perceptions as to the value of the Peer Observation Process as an effective means of professional development. Section II focused on Peer Observation and the collaborative process. Section III focused on the teachers' individual feelings and comfort level as a participant in the Peer Observation Process. Frequency distributions were collected for each section. The results were favorable. The large majority of teachers in the building felt that it was a worthwhile endeavor. All teachers, or 100%, felt that novice teachers were well served through Peer Observation, with 77% agreeing that veteran teachers could also be served through this process. Of the respondents, 85% felt that the process would improve one's teaching skills.

The respondents were basically in agreement when asked if they felt that Peer Observation was a beneficial form of professional development, with 82% agreeing and 9% strongly agreeing. These data are represented in Figure 3.1, with a 1 denoting *strongly disagree*, a 2 denoting *disagree*, a 3 denoting *undecided*, a 4 denoting *agree*, and a 5 denoting *strongly agree*.

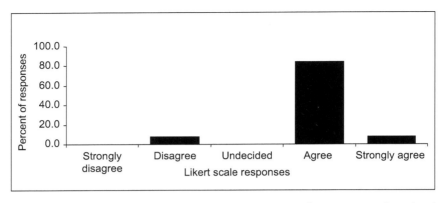

Figure 3.1 Teacher Response to Survey Question 7: Peer observation is a beneficial form of ongoing professional development.

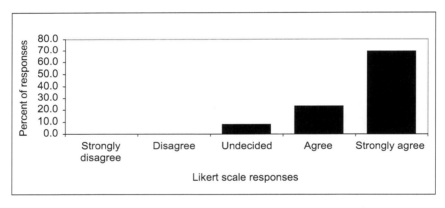

Figure 3.2 Teacher Response to Survey Question 12: It is important that the unique gifts, talents, knowledge, and expertise of each member of a Peer Observation Team be acknowledged and valued.

When evaluating the collaborative process in terms of Peer Observation, 92% felt that all team members should share equally in the professional growth for the team. As depicted in Figure 3.2, 69.2% of the respondents strongly agreed that each team member's individual talents and strengths be honored, 23% agreed as well. Conversely, as displayed in Figure 3.3, teachers felt strongly that teachers should share the same philosophies in order to have successful collaboration.

Collectively, teachers all agree that clear, open communication and clear expectations understood by all team members were imperative for successful collaboration with 100% and 92% in agreement respectively. Also,

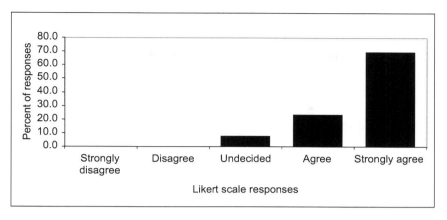

Figure 3.3 Teacher Response to Survey Question 13: Peer Observation Team members should share the same educational philosophy.

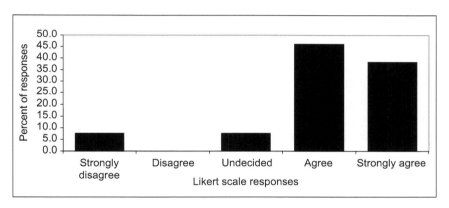

Figure 3.4 Teacher Response to Survey Question 32: I am comfortable with the concept of Peer Observation and support it as an effective means of professional development.

92% agreed that a strong commitment to the process was imperative for successful collaboration.

In Section III, 92% agreed that both a culture of open communication and shared leadership for professional development would increase the comfort level for the process; 92% of the respondents disagreed that it was hard to imagine having a colleague observe them teaching in the classroom. In terms of embracing the Peer Observation as an effective means of professional development, the results were mixed. According to Figure 3.4, 8% Strongly disagreed that they were comfortable with the Peer Observation Process used as an effective means of professional development; 45% agreed that

Peer Observation was an effective means for professional development with 38% strongly agreeing according to the survey.

While most agreed that this process would benefit both novice and veteran teachers, they were not in agreement as to Peer Observation being the best form of professional development; 75% agreed or strongly agreed that the Peer Observation Process would improve one's teaching skills. The majority of teachers agreed or strongly agreed that participants should be committed to the process, that the individual talents must be honored, and that teachers need not share the same methodologies or teaching techniques. Finally, 69.3% of respondents stated that they supported Peer Observation as an effective means for professional development.

Effect Size for Student Achievement

After two years, a statistical analysis was done to look at the student achievement on state mandated assessments. The effect size was calculated to determine if the program had made a difference on the state assessment in both reading and writing. An effect size is used to determine how effective an intervention has been when comparing two sets of data. Historically, the effect size magnitudes have been interpreted using Cohen's rule of thumb, where an effect size of .02 is considered small, approximately .05 is considered medium, and anything over .08 is considered large (Hill, Bloom, Black, & Lypsey, 2007). One might argue that instead of using a "one-size-fits-all" benchmark for determining the effect size, perhaps it would be better to measure effect sizes in accordance to the specific intervention used, the target population, and the final outcome. Kane (2004) did an empirical study to determine typical effect sizes in education. Kane's study followed student achievement scores from year to year ranging from kindergarten to 12th grade. Test scores from seven different nationally normed reading tests were used in the study. Each test's technical manual was used to interpret the mean score and student-level standard deviation by grade (Kane, 2004). In this empirical study, it was found that the elementary grades had a higher effect size in growth from year to year than the secondary grades. For example, the average annual reading gain from 1st to 2nd grade is a 0.97 *SD* whereas from 10th to 11th grade it decreases to a 0.19 (Kane, 2004). This study would tend to suggest, therefore, that using Cohen's measurement for determining the magnitude of an effect size would not be appropriate when used in studying student achievement in education.

The 2010 reading and writing state assessment for the research project had a sample size of 65. This group served as the control group for the research. The population consisted of students who were 66% Hispanic and 34% Caucasian. The mean score for reading for this group was 658.1 with a standard deviation of 66.7. The 2011 reading assessment had a sample size of 62, with a mean score of 672.2 and a standard deviation of 39.1. This group's scores served as the intervention group. The demographics were the same in terms of race. The effect size for reading based on the means and standard deviations of these two years' scores was 0.29.

For writing, the 2010 scores had a mean of 543.7 with a standard deviation of 70.80. The 2011 test scores had a mean of 551.39 with a standard deviation of 43.08. The computed effect size for writing was .13.

If one were to interpret these effect sizes according to Cohen's rule of thumb, then it could be assumed that the effect size was small for both reading and writing. If one used Kane's study that concluded that effect size magnitudes depended on the circumstances, and according to the data, if the typical effect size in education for a secondary student is 0.19, then the 0.29 effect size for reading would be considered practically significant. Although the effect size in writing was not large by either criterion, there was definitely a positive effect. Therefore, in answer to the question in regards to effectiveness it could be concluded that while there was a practical significance in terms of effect size for reading, the effect size for writing, although positive, was not practically significant. The Peer Observation Process had a positive effect on student achievement at this rural high school. The program overall had been a success.

Moving to the Dual Language Elementary School

Conversely, the process was then introduced to the dual language elementary school for further implementation. Again, the team leaders who had worked at the high school up the mountain introduced the process. This school needed a different focus, one that concentrated on the instruction involved with teaching a second language. Initial professional development was given in terms of second language acquisition best instructional practices. A checklist was created defining what needed to be seen in each classroom in terms of this instruction. Some teachers were skeptical at first, but willing to try. Teams were selected and once again, the process was set into motion.

It took about six months before the teams began to trust each other enough to truly engage in authentic and honest conversations. At the end of the first school year, the elementary team members asked to remain in the same teams for the following year. These teachers felt that they had just begun to dig deeper into their instructional practices with their peers and they were beginning to see results. The teachers then began the second year in the same teams.

At the end of the second year the World-Class Instructional Design and Assessment (WIDA) results came in for the 3rd grade. The WIDA is given to all Colorado students whose first language is not English. It gauges students' fluency levels in English. Prior to POPs being implemented in this school, no 3rd grader had tested at the fluent level in English. Yet after two years of making second language instruction the priority and providing the professional development through the Peer Observation Process, seven children tested at the fluent level in the 3rd grade! This process was helping to change the instruction at this dual language elementary school and the teachers were driving the process themselves!

Where to Begin?

Administrative Support

So, how do you go about setting up such a process? First and foremost it requires administrative support. This support is necessary to provide the biggest resource necessary for success: time. Time is needed for the collaboration. Time is needed for the teachers to complete the observations. The time needs to be embedded within the context of professional learning communities. Also, master teachers are needed to lead the teams. Do you have enough of them in your buildings to lead teams of about six to eight teachers?

Focus

The next step would be to establish your school's focus or area of need. This process can be used successfully to implement any focus needed. At the high school, the focus was the Gradual Release of Responsibility Model of Instruction. At the dual language school, the focus was best instructional practices for teaching a second language. A very real focus for all administrators moving forward is the instruction involved with the implementation of the Common Core Standards. This process is the perfect vehicle to use within the context of a PLC to implement and provide ongoing support for any needed instructional change:

> Encouraging teachers within a school to observe each other, to plan together, and to adopt shared teaching methods can dramatically improve teaching and learning in a school. Good practices in one classroom can become school wide shared practices. This work can ratchet up the levels of teaching and learning in a school while establishing school wide systems for diffusion and good ideas. Meanwhile it can also build a culture of high expectations and professional study.
>
> (Calkins, 2012)

Creating Teams

The best way to establish teams is to allow teachers to self-select. Planning times should be reviewed. Because observations will be completed during this time, it is most desirable to have teachers observe during different hours throughout the day. Understandably, teachers that have a common planning time should not be on the same team if at all possible. It is also nice to have same content area teachers see each other's instruction, but at small schools this is not always possible. Your priority does not have to revolve around content. It can be on commonalities of instruction that should be utilized in any classroom, any content area.

Establishing Norms

Once teams have been established, it is a good idea to give the teams some time to establish some norms that will work for their group. Our groups began with an exercise to gauge the teachers' comfort level regarding this process. Each team member was given an index card with a circle drawn on it. Teachers were to mark a dot on the card indicating their comfort level, with the very center of the drawn circle indicating complete comfort. The further their dot was drawn from the center of the circle, the more uncomfortable their feelings with the process. A dot drawn out of the circle indicated extreme discomfort. Team members were then to share their card and discuss their trepidations with the team members. This was a great way to begin the process as honest conversations were required and feelings were acknowledged. As a show of good faith, the team leaders went first in the observation rounds.

We learned a lot in the beginning of the process. One lesson that was learned was to ask the teacher being observed how he/she wanted to receive the feedback. What would make him/her most comfortable? It was helpful to first ask the teacher at the feedback session how he/she felt things went. Often the teacher would introduce the very area that needed help and the observing teachers could then offer suggestions. This approach felt safer for many teachers. The conversations were navigated using a series of questions and responses. Ideas and reflections about team members' teaching began to "popcorn" around the group. The energy level was raised and teachers became excited.

Every team seemed to have a personality of its own. Not all teams operated in exactly the same way. Each group found a format that worked for the members. The teachers were not only completely in charge of their own professional development, but they were driving the process as well. The teachers were, indeed, the experts.

One day during this collaborative time, it was noticed that the weather was quickly deteriorating with a blowing snowstorm coming in. When told that the meeting was going to be cut short so that all teachers could get safely home, one team answered by saying, "We'll be fine driving home. We're in a very rich part of our conversation and no one wants to leave just yet. Give us 20 more minutes to finish and then we'll leave!" When was the last time teachers were so engaged in conversations about instruction that they did not even want to leave during a blowing snowstorm? Does this process energize and motivate teachers? I think the answer is "yes"!

In conclusion, this process requires very few resources to implement and sustain. It demands a dedication to the process and time to participate. There is no better bargain financially for such powerful and evolutionary professional development. And the beauty of this process is that it can be tailored to fit the needs of any school, any focus.

4 | **Success**

The Peer Observation Process (POP) has contributed to success in a few key areas, such as test scores, school culture, and professionalism. What is more important is how POP acts as a vehicle for defining success and maintaining that success. As we discussed in the introduction, POP is a process rather than an answer. Embedded in your total professional development strategy is POP's ability to include the entire faculty in shared goal setting and shared support for increased performance. In this chapter, we discuss POP's role in defining success and maintaining success. We will describe success stories in the areas of test scores, school culture, and professionalism.

Since POP is a process, it's more about defining and maintaining. But what about what it *contributes* to success? In Chapter 1, we asked you to imagine a time-lapsed video of Friday morning collaboration meetings from the start of the Peer Observation Process to the start of its third year. Over time, the mood changed at these meetings as faculty worked more as a team than a group of individuals who had a classroom to run. Let's return to that image and zoom in a little to the baked goods. Yes, teachers started bringing baked goods to share with the entire staff. It seemed to be true that when you want people to get excited for meetings, try serving food. The very thought of Blueberry Boy Bait sent an early morning hustle to the library. In addition, we started celebrating important milestones by having the cafeteria staff whip up a delicious buffet of eggs, muffins, sausage, and coffee. Cooking with grease, folks! Test scores were edging up, we received a Governor's Award for achievement, and breakfast is served.

Four Success Drivers

It turns out that sharing food was not just about baked goods and eggs. It was about the Peer Observation Process. There was another kind of food being shared and it was a reason for success. Within the Peer Observation groups, teachers were sharing feedback, objectives, options, and decision making—F.O.O.D. We believe these to be four "success drivers" inherent in the process. They are the four things administration and leadership should pay attention to most when nurturing the program. Again, the four success drivers are: *Shared* . . . (1) **F**eedback (2) **O**bjectives (3) **O**ptions (4) **D**ecision making. "Shared F.O.O.D." is the constant element contributing to success in the Peer Observation Process.

Feedback

We've often noted that one of the great things about POP is that it has teachers using the very same methods found in the classroom to increase student performance for professional improvement. One of those things is feedback, the first shared success driver. Great teachers give great feedback and great professional environments include feedback. In 2007, John Hattie and Helen Timperley, of the University of Auckland, wrote "The Power of Feedback" in an edition of the *Review of Educational Research*. Hattie and Timperley state, "A teacher or parent can provide corrective information, a peer can provide an alternative strategy, a book can provide information to clarify ideas, a parent can provide encouragement, and a learner can look up the answer to evaluate the correctness of a response" (Hattie & Timperley, 2007). The Peer Observation Process routinely has teachers reviewing lessons and classroom practices together in an effort to move forward with what is working the best.

Feedback's effectiveness has a lot to do with other factors including timing, pre-established relationships, delivery style, and actual content. Feedback can be used for critical review of someone's performance or it can be used for positive reinforcement of desired performance. We will address the how-tos of feedback in POP later on in the logistics chapter. As a success driver, we highlight the emphasis of the Peer Observation Process on *peer* feedback, not *evaluative* feedback (from a supervisor).

POP offers faculty an outlet to intentionally improve performance on a continual, consistent basis with peers. This is in contrast to a biannual or annual evaluation from a supervisor. Indeed, teachers are practicing and honing their craft all year through micro-reviews from supportive peers. Success at schools sometimes feels hard to drive because adjusting practices in the classroom takes a long time to do. Feedback in the form of evaluations is too infrequent, and at that point, the ineffective practice could have been going on for a long time. We find many teachers enjoy the continual attention to their professional practice POP offers and benefit from the ownership the peer-driven process provides. Targeted areas get observed, feedback is immediately given, and opportunity for correction can happen the next day (or that afternoon). Improved performance, at least in one specific area, can be seen in a few months.

Objectives

The second success driver is shared objectives. A fully functioning Peer Observation Process, complete with full administration support, includes teachers' empowerment to set targets together. POP is a vehicle inside the system to continually empower teachers to position their practices to meet overall the school mission and goals. Teachers become part of the defining of success rather than the recipients of a top-down decision. The benefit is twofold with success not only in a targeted area (test scores), but also in school culture and professionalism. The staff becomes more motivated by the chance to take part in strategy formulation and implementation.

Administrators may relate the shared objectives concept to the "management by objectives," or "MBO," strategy made popular by leadership guru Peter Drucker. We asserted in earlier chapters that POP assists administrators in providing a focus in a particular area of professional development and building a positive professional culture. Peer groups taking ownership of goal setting works to do just that. Robert Kreitner and Angelo Kinicki in *Organizational Behavior* state, "A meta-analysis of MBO programs showed productivity gains in 68 of 70 different organizations. Specifically, results uncovered an average gain in productivity of 56% when top management commitment was high" (Kreitner & Kinicki, 2013).

Shared objectives drive success because they offer a balance to the overall skill development of teachers. Improved performance comes from a mix of what are called "performance outcome goals" and "learning goals" (Kreitner & Kinicki, 2013). Performance evaluations from supervisors may include both but usually emphasize the former. In the context of POP, shared objectives are learning goals because the feedback associated with the shared objectives is non-evaluative. Learning goals are defined as ones that "encourage learning, creativity, and skill development" (Kreitner & Kinicki, 2013). In *Organizational Behavior*, Kreitner and Kinicki explain why learning goals are important, "for employees who lack the necessary skills, performance outcome goals are more frustrating than motivating. When skills are lacking, a developmental process is needed wherein learning goals precede performance outcome goals" (Kreitner & Kinicki, 2013).

"Skills are lacking" may be cringe-inducing words because, yes, teachers and administrators are getting the brunt of this talking point in current education debates. Think, though, how POP addresses this head on. The "skills are lacking" line keeps coming up because the only measure being talked about are "performance outcome goals." The rate of change is so fast even veteran teachers are being asked to accomplish things that may be new for their current skill set. And they are only being measured by the end product. POP makes learning goals a serious part of professional development and recognizes that all teachers, not just new ones, need to update their skill set. Shared objectives within a peer group create a supportive environment of learning goals to assist all teachers in improving performance.

Options

The third success driver is shared options. This is perhaps the most fun success driver because, with gusto it brings out, wonderful teacher attributes such as goal orientation, perfectionism, and intellectual curiosity. Schools really hum when teachers are relentless in facilitating student success through new and challenging lessons. At the rural high school, teachers were talking about getting the lesson "perfect" for students. Good luck, right! Seriously, though, perfectionism can turn ugly and unproductive in an unstructured environment; the quest to find it can be fun. Teachers started searching and passing around electronic copies of articles and white papers about instructional strategies. The Principal sent out emails every Friday with four or five links and other teachers were encouraged to do the same at anytime. The school was brimming with ideas! Why? Because POP was a system that spread ideas like wild fire and encouraged more to be uncovered.

Cliché alert! Success and positive change don't come from doing the same old thing over and over again. Faculty and staff need to challenge thinking and practice new things tied to new goals and mandates. Of course, in an unstructured manner it would be chaotic. However, POP offers a structured system to appropriately share new ideas, practice them, and improve them based on feedback. Shared options highlight the dual learning that comes from Peer Observation. Not only is the observed teacher learning from feedback, but also the observer is learning new strategies from colleagues. This success driver emphasizes that success doesn't just come from correction and redirecting but simply from spreading the good ideas.

Filling pockets of instruction was most likely best achieved because of shared options. The star performers were opening their doors and discussing what was working. The good practices were being shared. Many times the peer groups would spend significant time on "have you tried this." The peer groups encouraged discussion of specific student groups and allowed teachers to approach whole grade levels with a unified strategy. Often times, as you know, grade levels move through a school with some shared attributes and the more teachers share the options of instruction that are working best, the better.

Decision Making

The fourth success driver is shared decision making. Again, decision making is closely aligned with shared objectives and the overall strategy of "management by objectives." POP is the vehicle for teachers to make daily decisions about what is working, what is not, and what needs to be done. They do it with the support and feedback of peers. POP is an embedded system providing autonomy to teachers. Let's be blunt, it removes a culture of micromanagement. Daniel Pink (2009) in *Drive* talks about autonomy, or "the desire to direct our own lives," as a major source of motivation. Administrators can use POP to communicate trust that the teachers are getting the job done on a daily basis. Teachers' professionalism is recognized and felt.

Autonomy and trust present in school culture will lead to success. Star performers will want to stay at your school because they are benefiting professionally. New teachers will learn more quickly through experimentation and intentional practice. According to the Center for Creative Leadership, 70% of adult learning takes place through challenging assignments, 20% takes place through coaching and mentoring, and 10% takes place in formal training (Rabin, 2013). It could be said that POP and all of its aspects accounts for 90% of organizational learning because it's a system for on-the-job training and mentoring and coaching. Shared decision making is a welcomed challenge for teachers as they work together to problem solve mistakes and chart new initiatives. The same CCL white paper of which we are referring talks about "action learning" as one way to "blend" the 90% and 10% of development techniques. It says:

> Action Learning projects are real work, not case studies or academic exercises. These projects are chosen with team and stakeholder involvement to have maximum impact for the organization. At the same time, they are opportunities for reflection, coaching, practice, and discussion of leadership skills and what it takes to be effective in the actual job environment.
>
> (Rabin, 2013)

That sounds like POP overall and the shared decision making specifically drives intimate involvement with "workplace experiences" (Center for Creative Leadership, 2).

In addition, shared decision making assists in making sense of dense data. The peer groups can go through state test scores one piece at a time, set shared objectives and decide together a strategy for meeting those objectives. They then share options, allow for individuals to decide what they will try, and conclude with shared feedback about how it is all going.

All four of the success drivers overlap with each other. The continuous shared feedback can be tied to shared objectives and include options. The feedback can address the implementation of shared decisions about strategy. POP success drivers do not address all aspects of school success and it does not act as a standalone solution. POP also needs high support from administration. POP does, however, provide an ongoing tool for school buildings to have continual, low cost professional development that is targeted and aligned.

Five Core Questions

The Peer Observation Process assists with alignment and definition of success because it not only helps with answers, but also surfaces the right ongoing questions. We think there are five core questions to answer when defining success. When the answer is no, POP, and its success drivers, acts as a vehicle to address the gap. When the answer is yes, POP acts as a maintenance device. The five core questions are: (1) Is the focus in the classrooms directly tied to the school mission and values? (2) Is the focus in the classrooms directly tied to explicit school strategic goals? (3) Is there an environment where teachers can develop and innovate classroom practices outside an evaluation from supervisors? (4) Do the faculty and staff have the opportunity to see the impact from their individual efforts on the collective success of the school? (5) Do teachers engage in healthy debate and critical feedback sessions aimed to drive positive improvement?

Identifying these five core questions as the critical components of defining success comes from the benefit of hindsight. The Peer Observation Process developed in response to a specific strategic goal of providing consistent, quality instruction in all classrooms for all students—"filling the pockets." It was after a year or two of practice that it became clear the process was contributing to other components of success. Then POP's move into an elementary school and middle school further cemented its role as a major contributor to success in five broad categories. Using it to address a specific strategic goal (like consistent instruction) seemed too narrow as comfort with the process allowed it to be used more sys-temically. That is why we talk about POP's contribution to success in test scores, culture, and professionalism. At this point, we also would purport that a school can customize the success they are looking for and use POP as a vehicle to get there. The five questions set a boundary in which POP works best.

Mission

The first question is less about a literal mission statement, although we suggest an updated one is extremely helpful for success, and more about establishing commonalities among the staff and administrators. Take the current language "college and career ready" as an example of mission. In POP, teachers take the time to really think about what that means for stu-dents in relation to current reality. Students are preparing for a transition of some kind at the end of every level (elementary to middle, middle to high school, high school to college and career). What does that student, or ahem . . . product, look like? Where is the compass pointing? These con-versations should be taking place in faculty meetings. POP goes to work reinforcing the values and actions tied to the common mission. It is not smooth or quick by any means and that is precisely why it works. Instead of enacting change in one single mandate, change comes in incremental doses regulated by the consistent meeting of teachers to discuss what is happening in the classroom.

Teachers won't be asked to change what they believe or who they are as a person with a broad stroke. That is recipe for revolt. They will, however, engage in reflecting on the successes (or lack of) of their practices. Through observation, they will see for themselves practices that are working and practices that are not working. They will receive supportive feedback. Perhaps the school collectively holds the value of high expectations. That may mean different things to different people. POP helps the staff to collectively calibrate what it means through the success drivers.

Talent Management

Answering this first question and using POP to define it or maintain it indirectly contributes to talent management, which is critical for sustained success. Imagine sitting in an interview with a great candidate. Credentials and accomplishments are there. Values are aligned. The candidate asks at the end of the interview, "So, what are you all about here at . . .?" You'll answer using language from your shared mission and values. But it doesn't stop there because if that star performer takes the job and doesn't see evidence of that mission and those values actually happening on a daily basis, you will lose her. The POP maintains pressure on the practice that of which is preached. Star performers also want to work with other star performers. The Peer Observation Process has teachers working alongside one another constantly talking about mission and values and how that looks in the classroom. Yes, over time it becomes clear that some individuals are not on the same page and don't plan to be. The POP gives these struggling teachers every opportunity to develop and grow around a common mission. Some will willingly leave for a different school. This kind of turnover is OK as all schools want people who want to be there. The everyday kind of articulation of mission and values happening in the POP allows someone to decide whether it's the place for them more quickly.

Strategic Goals

The second question is more cut and dry. The consistent observation process and feedback associated with each observation fills and broadens the pockets in specific areas. Is it consistent good instruction you need across all teachers? Is it increasing the amount of writing across content areas? Is it improved differentiation strategies for integrated IEP students? The administrator and instructional leaders can make a connection of daily classroom action to overall strategy and then measure whether it's working through the POP groups.

The POP helps clear the clutter of competing goals. POP is a face-to-face interaction among staff that reinforces what is important on a weekly basis. Administrators can announce at a faculty meeting or send out in an email a desired goal, but they are always faced with two main problems: A new habit doesn't stick without reinforcement and secondary goals dilute the fidelity of the primary ones. As the quote from an administrator in this book states, "We used to spend a lot of time talking about dress code, now we talk about instruction." Teachers deal with a lot of pulling forces that result in moving them further and further from a target that directly contributes to success. Eat or not eat in the classroom? Headphones or no headphones? The POP helps teachers stay focused on the true strategic goals, usually directly related to instruction, and they do this with the support of peers.

Strategic goals happen on the micro-level as well. Individual teachers drive their own observation and feedback. Perhaps they want to focus solely on transitions between lessons in the classroom. All the observers will focus on that and surgically address that challenge area. Teachers can use the process to meet larger strategic professional goals in manageable pieces. Teachers have reported feeling more prepared for evaluations from supervisors because the Peer Observation group had been providing support and feedback about certain lessons all along.

Professional Learning Environment

The third question is directly related to the Peer Observation Process. In an environment of such rapid change, teachers need more support when developing and practicing. Teachers are practicing education in the same way doctors are practicing medicine. Success will not come when every action is an endgame with an evaluative outcome. POP allows teachers to take calculated risks, confront challenges head on, and stretch creativity in the classroom. These three things done at appropriate levels instigate the innovation needed to move forward the field of education.

Noticeable Impact

The fourth question is too often neglected or taken for granted in education. Teachers don't have quarterly reports to cheer about, or monthly sales figures, or other kinds of really visible success. Even test scores leave a little to be desired when searching for something to display individual contribution to results, especially for teachers outside of the core content areas. We are talking about "task identity," defined by Kreitner and Kinicki as "the extent to which the job requires an individual to perform a whole or completely identifiable piece of work. In other words, task identity is high when a person works on a product or project from the beginning to end and sees a tangible result" (Kreitner & Kinicki, 2013, p. 228). A lot of times teachers do not even feel they are working on a "project," rather it is a never-ending journey towards an unidentifiable end. Second, they almost rarely have time to sit down and review results in detail and discuss how the results were directly tied to individual actions. POP addresses these two issues.

First, POP breaks down teaching to projects. A strategic goal aligned with a mission is set, and then the group establishes shared objectives, shares options to get there, makes decisions, and provides feedback as to how it is going. When data become available, like state test scores, the POP group is able to digest the scores by relating them to the specific strategic goal and what they did to contribute to it. Commitment to POP means commitment to time for collaboration. With POP, administrators have a structured time to review scores and data with fidelity and not feel like it is taking away from something else. This creates task identity.

Task identity is important for increased motivation and performance. Organizational behaviorists J. Richard Hackman and Greg Oldham identify task identity as one of the "core job characteristics" that plays a role in intrinsic motivation and the "critical psychological state" of "experienced meaningfulness of the work" (Kreitner & Kinicki, 2013). Another core job characteristic is "feedback from job," which leads to another "critical psychological state" of "knowledge of the actual results of the work activities" (Kreitner & Kinicki, 2013). POP is a way to systematically have teachers review data and scores otherwise too cumbersome to review with relevance.

Healthy Debate

You're on the road to success now with POP. The fifth question is about not remaining satisfied with short-term success and pushing for sustainable success at the core of the school culture. A fully functioning Peer Observation Process includes an established environment that supports healthy debate and critical feedback. This is not something you'll see right away but will be the indicator of deeper success.

Healthy debate goes back to the "calibration" mentioned around the first question. Shared mission and values comes from an appropriate level of conflict. It takes a bit of a struggle to get to shared meaning and an agreed path forward. POP provides a structured, professional outlet for this to take place. Feedback will be discussed at length in the logistics chapter. It's a success driver and core tenet of the Peer Observation Process. A culture of awareness and reflection is critical for sustained success.

As you know, you have to be relentless to create sustained success. Complacency and lost focus, even if for a short period of time, can cost months of growth. Teaching has got to be one of the hardest professions because of its constant motion and change. The students are there every day, rain or shine, during the change, policy mandates, lack of resources, etc. The Peer Observation Process is not the silver bullet that solves everything, but it is a continual process, always in motion, working for you to define and maintain success.

Success Stories

We're all familiar with the "big ticket" definition of success: Test scores. The stress levels increase around March as students across the country sit at desks with their #2 pencils and (we hope) demonstrate their learning. Then, we wait until July or August to dissect the results. Where did we grow? Where did we drop? Why?? We then meet as a staff to create goals for the following school year, based on results that are from students who may or may not be at the school anymore.

Schools recognize the inefficiency of that process. More and more buildings are creating and incorporating PLCs to help alleviate that very inefficiency. However, as mentioned earlier, the data can seem daunting to many staff. They are seen not as a tool to drive improvement but as a reminder of what went wrong the previous year.

Each of the three specific schools was able to define success criteria that matched its individual building needs. The rural high school used POP as a way to increase the level of instruction throughout the building. The elementary school was wanting to better prepare teachers for the second language learners they would all have in their classrooms. The inner city middle school wanted to increase the levels of literate engagement in each of the classes. Each was able to do so, not through outside professional development, but through the intentional observation of their peers and strategic discussions afterwards. All of these goals will lead to improvements in the areas discussed earlier in this chapter.

The Rural High School

Test Scores

So how can you measure these results using test scores? Because let's face it, test scores are significant indicators of progress at a school, whether or not we agree with them. Let's start at the rural high school. As the CADI report had pointed out, quality instruction was lacking in many areas. This could be reflected in the low test scores that were earned year after year. However, after implementing the POP, TCAP scores went up. And the growth that was seen was not marginal by any means. When looking at the 2011 District Performance Framework, the high school met or exceeded growth expectations in *all three* content areas (reading, writing, math). The high school was the only school in the district to have scores that exceeded any of the expectations. As a result, the high school was awarded the Colorado Governor's Distinguished Improvement Award in both 2010 and 2011. Again, it was the only school in the district to be recognized. There were other factors at play here, sure. However, the POP served as the foundation for all of the successes that were occurring at the school.

Professionalism

One of those byproducts of the POP was an increased level of professionalism in the building. Teachers were holding each other accountable for what was going on in the classrooms. It was not necessarily common to have teachers showing movies on a regular basis, but, as recognized in the audit, the level of instruction was definitely not consistent. Then, all teachers became significant stakeholders. Teachers were regularly watching classes, making observations and taking notes. The teachers were also regularly discussing what was seen. These discussions, again, forced the staff to reflect on practices, thus raising the level of instruction in ALL classes, not just in the pockets where quality instruction was already found.

One of the key elements of this process is that it is done in a safe, almost nurturing environment. There were first-year teachers in groups with seasoned veterans. In some situations, this could almost be detrimental to both parties, as the veteran sees little value for the rookie's perspective. And likewise, the youngster could feel almost intimidated, unwilling to be critical as it might be seen as an insult. However, because POP was introduced and set up in a way that encouraged collaboration among peers, the vets ended up craving the feedback from their inexperienced partners. There was an implicit (and explicit, actually) understanding that this was not evaluative, nor would it ever become so. The walls that some naturally put up when receiving feedback were literally knocked down when that became clear. It wasn't judgmental. It was real professional development.

Culture

This ties, coincidentally enough, into school culture as well. Before 2009, there had been years of high turnover, sometimes over 50% of the staff. The culture itself was a major reason for many who left. It was no coincidence that once the program was initiated, turnover decreased dramatically. Again, there were other factors at play, but a satisfied staff will stay. Through POP, the staff became passionate about their environment. Why were they so satisfied? There are many intangibles that come along with this, as further witnessed at the other schools as well. However, through POP, teachers become empowered in their profession. In an age where many feel less and less like professionals, here they are told to make each other better. *Their administrators trust them.* With that trust comes more motivation to do the job well. When a staff is motivated and they believe in what they are doing, possibilities literally become endless.

There is a certain feel in schools when teachers like being there. If you were to walk through, you wouldn't necessarily be able to put your finger on it, but you would know it's there. That's how POP works. It brings with it a "feeling" that good things are going on. But it certainly goes beyond simply a feeling. As mentioned, there are concrete indicators that this process truly works. Those "pockets" of good instruction are spreading. And soon, all students are receiving high-quality instruction. And with that, teachers feel positive, optimistic.

Dual Language Elementary School

The second school to incorporate the POP was a dual language elementary school in a neighboring community. Again, the school scores were not what the district desired. And again, POP was implemented. This time the goal was to direct the focus to best instructional practices around second language acquisition. The measurement for this new focus would be both the WIDA, a test that assesses English acquisition, and the TCAP, or Colorado state assessment.

The POP was immediately introduced at the summer inservices. Teachers from the rural high school came down and walked the staff through the "hows and whys" of the program. The staff bought in right off the bat. They realized the value of peer collaboration as a means for improvement in all classrooms. For a new Principal, recognizing the professionalism already present in the building was a tremendous victory. There would be less energy spent on convincing teachers why this was a valuable process, and more spent on the school's goal. The POP further reinforced the relationships in the building. Again, from the start there was a trust coming from the new Principal to her staff, a loud message that the teachers would be treated as professionals. This trust is then repaid by a staff willing to work their hardest and do whatever it would take to get kids where they needed to be academically.

Test Scores

Reality dictates that schools must also look at the test scores to measure growth. At the elementary school, it was no different. This school also earned the Colorado Governor's Distinguished Improvement Award for three consecutive years. That's five years of POP at two different schools and five years of the prestigious growth award. That is not a coincidence. As a reminder, the school's main goal focused on second language learners and their growth on the WIDA test. During its implementation, students at the elementary school scored "proficient" on the WIDA exam *for the first time ever.* Also noted was the drop in turnover in staff. This alone would make most districts satisfied. However, through POP, it becomes the norm. There were other benchmarks attained as well as measured by growth throughout on the NWEA assessment and a continued growth on the state TCAP assessments.

Professionalism and Culture

As scores begin to improve at a school, the culture transforms as well. Several teachers at the school noted this, as we'll recount in subsequent chapters. The staff recognized the power of their POP group. They would regard the biweekly meeting time as sacred, not allowing other meetings or grading or even impending snowstorms to interrupt it. When a staff is this committed, the positive peer pressure "encourages" all to perform at their best. Teachers, again, do not want to let each other down. They come to the meetings prepared, ready to share feedback. They develop such a strong rapport that the feedback quickly becomes meaningful. Teachers begin to challenge each other to do better, to reflect on their work on a daily basis. When groups get to this level, we really see growth throughout the school.

Inner City Middle School

Let's move to the inner city middle school. This process started while the school was on year two of turnaround status. The previous school year, there was a brand new administration along with a near 50% rate of new teachers. Year one was spent "cleaning up" what had been going on for several years, which led to the turnaround status. During year one, scores went up in areas, stayed stagnant in areas, and went down in areas. Unfortunately, the school would not be leaving the turnaround status.

Professionalism and Culture

As year two approached, the Principal set up a schedule that would allow for the implementation of the POP. He was able to see how it was successful in the previous schools and had faith that it would also work at his school.

Like the previous year, the turnover going into year two was high, over 50%. There would be a handful of brand new teachers mixed in with those who had been teaching for five to 10 years plus. It was agreed that with such a mix of experience, it was a prime time to implement the POP.

As the school focus was being worked out, the school was receiving outside professional development from Dr. Kevin Feldman pertaining to the implementation of literate engagement strategies throughout the school. It was decided that when the Principal did informal walk-throughs, he would use the document presented at the training. It made sense, then, that the teachers use this same document for their observations as well. Immediately, that put teachers at ease.

Some background: For the veterans, they had been used to being "dinged" on walk-throughs by previous administrators. It was to the point where teachers were literally having anxiety attacks as a result. The environment was *not* one of trust. Teachers did not feel trusted as professionals at all. They were feeling micromanaged. The culture was not one of open feedback and growth. It was not one to encourage peers to come in, for fear of being criticized.

Immediately on implementation of POP, teachers were able to see its value. It started with the trust that was shown by administration. They explicitly agreed to stay out of the conversations and the observations. This established, from the get-go, that the POP was non-evaluative. The process was put into place to improve their teaching, to further develop their craft. This validation was all that the veteran teachers needed to give their buy-in. Once they realized that they wouldn't be "dinged" by their peers, doors began to open and conversations began to flow. For the brand new teachers, this served almost as a mentoring program. They had multiple opportunities to receive feedback and see instruction. Several have commented that they can't imagine starting off their careers and not having the POP to help. Honestly, it has been an invigorating process from the perspective that *everyone* in the building is talking about instructional practices.

Interviews with some of the teachers in later chapters will specifically give examples of how the level of professionalism has been raised at all locations. But again, walking through this school feels very familiar, as it's the same feeling experienced while walking through the rural high school. In every classroom, it's about instruction, not discipline, not dress code. While it's too soon to measure success here using test scores, the Colorado Department of Education has weighed in based on what they have seen. In a recent visit to the middle school, they stated that the middle school was seen as an exemplary school, particularly noting the high-quality teaching and learning taking place in the building.

Customized Success

As can be seen, each school has experienced success in multiple areas, those being test scores, school culture, and professionalism. While they each used a unique set of goals to measure, the POP was flexible enough to serve as the vehicle for all. One of the strengths of this process is that it takes on the form that the schools want. If you were to visit the three schools mentioned, they would all look different in how they implement the process. The documents are different, the meetings are different, the emphasis is different. The one key element they all have in common, however, is success.

5 | Keys to Communication

When was the last time you participated in a meeting, workshop, or training that discussed communication? It was probably recently and most likely several times before that. Communication is the most important foundation to all initiatives, hence the abundance of air time, however, it rarely gets attention as a primary focus. The Peer Observation Process relies on sound communication skills. The building leadership needs to consider ways to nurture a supportive environment and opportunities for skill development in the area of communication. Here, we would like to discuss some communication topics for you to consider when encouraging those meaningful conversations so necessary for a successful POP implementation.

Key and Padlock

There is a popular team-building activity found in the playfully titled "Raccoon Circles—A Guide for Facilitators" by Jim Cain in Brockport, NY. The activity is called "The Keys to Communication" (Cain, 2007). Dr. Cain quickly notes in the set-up: "This expanded version was first used with a team theme of trying to 'unlock the future'" (Cain, 2007). We love it! Here is how it goes: The facilitator first sets up a "playing area" in the shape of a rectangle. The participants are asked to split into two teams and gather around the boundaries of the rectangle, each team taking a side. Two volunteers, one from each team, are asked to step out into the playing area. The facilitator proceeds to blindfold each volunteer and ushers them to opposing ends of the playing area. At this point, he engages the crowd and reveals the task.

The facilitator holds up two objects: A key and a padlock. The objective is for each team to verbally explain to their volunteer where the keys and padlock are located and then to open the lock. Chaos ensues. The facilitator introduces Round 2 that incorporates some planning time for a new volunteer and teammates to discuss strategy. Then the activity is repeated and includes an optional Round 3 using a combination lock. Holding true to solid team-building initiative practice, the facilitator runs a debriefing session for the team to discuss communication (Cain, 2007).

Key #1: Time for Planning and Strategy

POP draws on several lessons from "The Keys to Communication." (If you are interested in a full explanation of the activity and others, more information can be found at www.teamworkandteamplay.com.) For now, the number one key to communication is time for planning and strategy. If the teacher that is being observed heads into the classroom on an observation day with no prior meeting or set up, the communication debrief and feedback session will be less effective and chaotic. Think about Round 1 compared to Round 2.

Time can be one of the bigger challenges for a successful POP implementation. Meeting times for the peer groups slowly experience a reduction as other topics and priorities become more urgent. It is easy to see the time groups spend chatting in person as less productive and a secondary focus. However, making in-person communication meeting times a primary focus increases productivity. Teams should be talking before and after observations to make the observation most targeted and therefore productive.

Time does something else very important. It builds the trust important for effective communication. POP really starts to work when the teams are having meaningful conversations. Meaningful conversations go beyond surface-level observations and the casual avoidance of tough feedback. To go deeper and experience a safe environment to share specific, tough feedback the groups need trust. The more time they spend together, both informally and formally, the more the group will become comfortable tackling the tough work. Resist the urge to shorten meeting times because a few members report that more socializing is taking place. Our experience at the high school was that in the beginning many groups socialized more than strategized, but over time the groups were feeling stressed to get everything reported and analyzed. The ownership and accountability began to rise as the group met and communicated more. As we all know, things we care about most get time. Time communicating is both simple and hard, but crucial to POP.

Building leaders will be met with two scenarios regarding time: (1) The bought-in staff will want more of it and (2) The less bought-in staff will want less of it. Listen to the former group and protect the meeting time of the POP teams. Time is key to communication; communication is key for planning and strategy; and planning and strategy is necessary for positive outcomes. If people are getting annoyed at how often things are said, things are going well. We rarely see feedback from employee surveys saying the leadership communicates too much and that there is too much time for communication within teams.

Key #2: Set Boundaries

A second lesson from "The Keys to Communication" is boundaries. As with all good activities, games, or sports, there are boundaries. In POP, the boundary is that the process of giving feedback is non-evaluative. The Peer Observation groups may need continuous reinforcement that what is observed and later said in feedback sessions is to be used solely for growth and reflection. Can you imagine the activity with the volunteer in the playing area searching around for the key and padlock as the other team members simultaneously shout instructions and log the mistakes they are making? What usually happens is that the team members start to imagine themselves in the playing area and get even more enthusiastic about helping because they would want the same. Teachers behave the same way in POP. They observe a colleague, learn things for their own classroom (for their turn), and provide feedback in an empathetic way. This happens when very clear boundaries are placed on conversations and communication. Remember to have team leaders of the peer groups emphasize and re-emphasize that the sessions are non-evaluative.

The other communication boundary appropriate for a successful Peer Observation session is having one or two objectives. We have indicated throughout this book that POP can be used to spread good practice in a number of areas, however, the focus should be limited for at least one cycle of Peer Observations. Most of you will take an entire year working on one aspect of improvement. Communication is most effective when the peer group is focused on a specific item of feedback. In the activity, the single focus is to have the volunteer open the lock. There are many individual steps to do just that, made more difficult because the volunteer is blindfolded (more on that in a moment). Again, can you imagine if team members were throwing in commentary about how the actual lock mechanism worked? It's in the ballpark, but not necessary at the moment. It was mentioned previously that POP's strategic drivers help "clear the clutter." That is made possible with effective communication and effective communication is specific and targeted within boundaries.

Key #3: Build Self-awareness

The third Peer Observation lesson from "The Keys to Communication" is awareness. One of the things that really enables meaningful conversations is the ability for the participants to talk openly about what they do know and what they do not know. When they feel comfortable and when they do not feel comfortable. In the activity, there is this idea of vulnerability enhanced by the blindfold. At least it is assumed that the volunteer has seen a key and padlock before and therefore has the awareness of the area of support. By the same token, the team members are all aware that the volunteer knows what a key and padlock look like, and how they relate to each other, he or she just does not know where they are located. We know when it comes to the classroom things are not as easy. Several nuances are introduced and awareness becomes more difficult.

Most people have difficulty talking about themselves, particularly when it comes to professional competency or incompetency. They may not know, or may not want to share, the area of need. Contrariwise, team members may not always be able to see what the person needs as it either can be subtle or clouded by perception bias. Communication of strengths and weaknesses is an essential part of Peer Observation. The feedback sessions become more and more powerful as the observed teachers take ownership of areas in which they need to grow. Empathy and trust rise as the team members learn the various areas of sensitivities and stress points among their colleagues.

So how can you nurture awareness as a key to communication? First, you make it a priority and consider how you are encouraging and rewarding self-awareness. Building leaders should model the behavior of simultaneously discussing areas of challenge (asking for help) and guiding in areas of strength. Second, facilitate meeting "jump-starts." Consider several Peer

Observation team meetings beginning with a roundtable go-around consisting of each member sharing one thing they did well this week and one thing that didn't go well. These little moments gather momentum and establish a culture of sharing. Consider also each team member making a line down a page and writing down topics they could teach other teachers on one side and topics they would like to learn on the other. Follow up by creating a schedule of teachers leading lessons for other teachers. It can be part of an overall professional development program and joins nicely with POP. I am sure you get the idea of what little questions or activities you can do to start meeting to develop an awareness culture. Increased self-awareness will make for more meaningful conversations.

Formal self-awareness tools, or assessments, are always an option as well. A major benefit of the Peer Observation Process is the little-to-no cost; however, if you do have a budget for professional development, consider a self-awareness tool. The use of such a tool comes with some tips and cautions. One, preparing a formal professional development session facilitated by a trained practitioner of a self-awareness tool indicates that you are serious about communication as a priority. Two, a tool provides a common language to everyone that can propel effective communication in a team at a faster rate.

In the area of caution: First, avoid taking any free online assessments. They typically lack sound psychometrics and assume that the report is the end result. In fact, the reports from assessments are only the beginning and a trained practitioner of the tool will facilitate deeper learning and understandings. Second, only do the assessment if you are committed to incorporating the language and learning into the culture of the school. Many of these tools have a bad reputation as unhelpful. Much of that is because the proper time is not invested. Remember that a one-day session rarely will be helpful long term. A tool is meant to work within or alongside something else more systemic, like the Peer Observation Process. This book is focusing on the Peer Observation Process and does not officially endorse any of these tools, however, here are few suggestions for you to explore later: (1) Standout™ by the Marcus Buckingham Company, is a "strengths-based" tool that is very practical and effective (has an online platform that is great for teams), (2) Myers-Briggs Type Indicator© (MBTI), published by CPP, Inc. is a long-established tool for self-awareness and requires a certified facilitator, and (3) the Hogan Assessment©, by the Hogan Assessment Systems, is an extensive tool with a suite of assessments and also requires a certified facilitator. No matter how you develop self-awareness, remember to include it as a key to communication and therefore an essential foundation to POP.

Key #4: Feedback

The fourth lesson we can draw from "The Keys to Communication" is feedback. Feedback is a component of good communication, as is listening, and is a POP "success driver." In the activity, the volunteer first receives feedback in an unstructured, chaotic manner. The facilitator simply tells the team to guide the volunteer to the key and padlock. The volunteer typically cannot hear anything because they hear everything. This is why the facilitator introduces planning time in the second round. As you might have guessed, some teams figure this out before Round 2 and identify one person to talk to the volunteer. During Round 2 the volunteer now knows to cue her listening to one voice. The challenge is the other team may be making a lot of noise. So, let's unpack this lesson.

The first idea is that we stick to the theme of paying attention to these things that can easily get pushed aside as we assume them to be "givens" or "soft skills." Feedback, as many of you know, can go very badly if not done right. Many of you have probably done some coursework or professional development sessions on giving feedback and continue to incorporate that learning during evaluations. In the Peer Observation Process, we want to approach feedback in a less evaluative manner. This peer support dynamic almost makes it more difficult because most people are less used to it. Peer coaching and support are not as prevalent as the manager–employee evaluation dynamic in most organizations.

Feedback Tips

The second thing you can do is incorporate specific feedback practices in your POP teams. During the first few years of this process, we learned some key things about feedback related to communication in the peer teams. The building leaders facilitating Peer Observation teams should consider these tips:

1 The observed teacher defines the focus of all the observations. This promotes the ownership of personal development and empowers the teacher as a professional. Consider how the awareness piece mentioned earlier plays into this. In a pre-meeting, the observed teacher has time to discuss with team members some of the things they are working on, what the lesson plans will broadly cover throughout the cycle, etc. This

will avoid instances of someone giving feedback unrelated, too sensitive at the moment, and/or out of context. We know that when you walk into a classroom once it is hard to have the whole story. Allow the observed to give a set up for context and direction for feedback.

2 When the observation cycle is completed and it is time for the observed teacher to receive feedback, let him report first how the lessons went. The team can remind them which days and classes were observed but allow for him to have airtime first. POP is meant to increase professionalism and this is an aspect that contributes to that. Many teachers know exactly how a class went. Offer them the time to reflect and communicate their own feelings. A simple boundary to offer for this communication is the "plus and delta" debrief model. Having a simple tool is very useful for those who have less comfort reflecting verbally about their performance. The "plus and delta" model is so widespread on the internet it is hard to even cite a specific source.

3 The observed teacher should have the choice of how they receive the feedback. This suggestion involves a slight nuance. We feel that there should always be a full team debrief of the observation cycle. The team aspect is part of the experience that increases professionalism, collaboration, and creativity. However, the observed teacher should have the option to receive more sensitive feedback in another setting if they choose. Incorporating one of the self-awareness "jump-starts" can aid this aspect of feedback. A team member can discuss with the other team members that receiving difficult feedback is very uncomfortable and is willing to receive it but prefers it to be one on one. Another complexity is the idea of feedback in writing. We would offer the suggestion that difficult feedback can be in writing but should include a face-to-face meeting to review the written document. Remember that POP is meant to bring teachers together and feedback solely through email and/or written documents will reduce the impact. Indeed, this is referring to more sensitive, critical feedback and does not replace the process set-up of an observation form.

These three feedback practices are simple yet powerful. Use them as a set-up or orientation to POP. Notice the focus on direct communication, boundaries, reflection of self, and respect. The last step you can take is to introduce some feedback models you like to the entire staff as part of a support system for the overall Peer Observation Process. The internet is chock full of feedback models, using acronyms, steps, etc. to act as a guide. Consider empowering a staff member to research and lead a short workshop. Indeed, this can be coupled with learning about giving student feedback. We will provide two quick suggestions for feedback models here and note customization for the Peer Observation Process. We would like to emphasize, however, the opportunity to have staff involved in choosing and learning a model. The ownership will increase buy-in.

Feedback Models

One feedback model comes from MIT's Human Resources Department. It happens to align nicely with POP's objectives because the language can be easily used regarding professional practice in a classroom. Keep in mind the boundary of non-evaluative, professional feedback. Many models include sharing your personal feelings. They have their place, particularly when team building within the peer teams, but effective feedback in POP is focusing on professional practice and is more about how the students respond, lessons were received, etc. MIT's Human Resources (n.d.) has a "Four-Part Model":

(1.) Context: Describe the situation; give feedback in a timely manner, (2.) Behavior: Describe the behavior as clearly as possible, as if you were watching a movie; avoid drawing conclusions, (3.) Impact: What were the results—positive or negative—of this behavior?, (4.) Next Steps: What specific behavior should be changed or repeated in response to the feedback; why should this change be made. (Massachusetts Institute of Technology, 2013)

In regards to number 4: In the context of the Peer Observation Process, the feedback should use language like "consider" or "might I suggest," and a lot of "what do you think?" Providing next steps in a strong manner crosses the boundary of non-evaluative. The feedback sessions should air on the side of giving the observed plenty of time to personally reflect.

Here is another feedback model that is a little more blunt but maintains ownership with the observed teacher with the use of the word "I". The model is "Stop-Keep-Start (SKS) Doing" model designed by Phil Daniels of

Brigham Young University and discussed in a *Harvard Business Review* blog post by Thomas Delong. The model has the feedback seeker ask team members these three questions: "(1) What should I stop doing? (2) What should I keep doing? (3. What should I start doing?" We think these three questions are really powerful and could produce great gains. We also think that this model could be introduced after POP has been running for a while and trust has been established or you simply have a group that is a little more eager to cut to the chase. Later in the blog, comes a great description of the power of this tool:

> The SKS also counteracts our tendency to avoid seeking out other people's opinions of our attitudes and behaviors. When you are feeling the worst about yourself, you don't ask for more feedback. You don't want to know. You use the excuse that you are already being tough on yourself, so you don't need anyone else to be harsh. This rationale creates a vicious cycle where there is no need for you to learn of other views or ask for help. If you don't hear the hard truth from others, you don't have to acknowledge that it's real. The SKS process breaks the hold our illusions have on us.

Right now, we have communication as an important foundation to a successful Peer Observation Process. We view communication, not as a "soft skill" or "a given" or "complementary," but rather something requiring regular attention and priority. We can remember some "keys" while making communication a priority: Schedule plenty of time for it to happen, set clear boundaries of what should be discussed and how, increase opportunities to build self-awareness, and establish feedback practices and use models for giving it. These things will be great as they have worked and will work. However, you still need to prepare for conflict. In fact, you need to prepare the teams to encourage and engage in healthy conflict. Why? Because the more your teams are able to handle difficult conversations in the form of tough, critical feedback, the more performance improvement you will see.

Having Difficult Conversations

In the first year of POP at the rural high school in Colorado, a new teacher observed a veteran teacher. The class didn't go well and both the new teacher and veteran teacher knew it. But how would it come up in the feedback session that coming Friday? Thus far each feedback cycle in this particular group had included mostly glowing praises. This was not a bad thing. It was sign of a positive, collegial work team. However, the mantra of POP was to improve classroom practices and provide feedback to colleagues to direct the improvement. There was always going to be something positive to say but that was not always going to be the thing to drive improvement. The new teacher had to have a difficult conversation.

Some obvious thoughts came into play for the young teacher: "Who am I to tell her how to teach . . . She has been teaching for 10 years . . . It's not worth it to say anything because I alone can't change it . . . I have to see her every day, I don't want it to be awkward." The young teacher sat at his desk and remembered some of the set-up language for the Peer Observation groups, the very words shared earlier in this chapter. He remembered that there was, in fact, some history and trust with this veteran teacher and knew that could be the positive foundation of a difficult conversation. In addition, the young teacher had leadership aspirations and knew giving feedback was an important aspect. It was because of this, too, that he felt loyal to the fidelity of the program.

The young teacher wrote his feedback in writing paying particular attention to writing the language to be objective and coldly observational without judgment. He printed the sheet and headed down to the teacher's room, knowing she was on her planning period. "You and I both know that the lesson I observed didn't go well. I'm sorry about that. What's been going on lately?" It was from there the two talked about what was going on and some areas to focus on immediately to get things back on track. The veteran teacher had changed content areas and was feeling a little overwhelmed. The veteran teacher did most of the talking and thanked the young teacher for his candidness and respect. When it came time for the team to meet on Friday, the young teacher simply said he had discussed things with the veteran teacher prior. Many nodded and things moved forward.

We know that feedback can be real easy when it's "good job," "nice, fun lesson," etc. We also know that sometimes feedback can be hard to deliver when the observation turned up some difficult conversations to be had. In order to have an effective Peer Observation group, the group must be willing to engage in these difficult conversations. It is not always helpful when we sit around a table and tell each other how great we are. Encourage your staff that difficult conversations are indeed more of a sign of respect than not having them. If they are not being had then it means people do not care and are not secure enough to confront challenges in the relationship.

Will your POP roll out with everyone diving in for some meaty critical feedback? No. That is OK because trust and some relationship building has to happen first. But do not let it go on too long. The building leaders should be modeling feedback that includes areas of challenge.

Difficult conversations will also come from differences in opinions, philosophies, and protectiveness of ideas. The elementary school utilized a communication and conflict tool in a facilitated workshop for teachers looking to conduct more meaningful conversations in their peer groups. The tool was called the Strength Deployment Inventory© (SDI), based on Elias Porter's relationship awareness theory. The teachers were able to think about what their motivations and strengths are both when things are going well and when they are in conflict. Once the peer groups were able to connect more on a motivation level ("I want my students to succeed"), they were able to have difficult conversations about specific teaching behaviors without being threatened ("Yes, now I see that I can be more flexible in assignment options for higher level students"). We mentioned a few tools for self-awareness earlier in this chapter. The "SDI" accomplishes several goals including managing interpersonal conflict. Check out Personal Strengths Publishing, Inc., based in Carlsbad, CA, for more information (again, we do not officially endorse this tool). Encourage healthy debate and view conflict as a tool for improvement as it often yields new thinking and thrilling engagement.

Conclusion

Nurturing communication takes a lot of effort and happens to be more of a skill than natural practice. The tools, models, and practices are abundant. Take some time to develop a communication strategy for POP. Perhaps the peer groups could tackle communication goals and expected norms as an early project. Communication is a core element of the Peer Observation Process and will prove to be the key to "unlock the future."

6 | So What About the Common Core?

A single conversation across the table with a wise person is worth a month's study of books.

(Chinese proverb)

Regardless of your feelings about Common Core, many states have made the commitment to implement with fidelity. The biggest shift in Common Core is not the "what" we are to teach, but rather "how" to instruct at this rigorous level (Peterson, 2013). Have these state leaders put much thought into the professional development needed to proceed successfully? Some districts have done a nice job; others, not so much. Certainly the "Here are the standards . . . now go teach them," method will be found to be sorely lacking.

The Principal, with the support of the district and state, will be the key to the success of the standards. Study after study points to the Principal as the single key to a strong school culture (MetLife, 2013). As the Principal, you will be responsible for a successful implementation of this curriculum if your state has adopted the Common Core State Standards (CCSS). You should ask yourself:

- Have I set a vision for the transition to the implementation of the Common Core State Standards?

- What is my plan to give teachers the tools they need to succeed?

- Have I created buy-in for such a plan?

- How will I provide ongoing support once the plan is set in motion?

The Common Core requires instructional changes that are not found in the document itself. Students will be required to perform at a higher level, defend their thinking, and provide evidence of their conclusions. Nowhere does the Common Core tell teachers how to teach to realize student achievement at this level. "I predict the common-core standards will fail, unless we do massive professional development for teachers." Hung-His Wu goes on to say, "There is no fast track to this" (Frenkel & Wu, 2013). So, what are schools to do?

School leaders have learned much about what constitutes good instruction but have yet to create highly effective instructional systems. Traditionally, school leaders have focused on building individual capacity and attempted to improve teaching one teacher at a time, and they must continue to do that (MetLife, 2013). School leaders can build individual capacity by carefully recruiting and hiring staff who are first and foremost team players. But they must also work like musical conductors, bringing out the best across the entire ensemble using systems approaches, such as instituting problem-based learning structures. The new standards mean that teamwork, both within the school and among schools, must become a nonnegotiable (MetLife, 2013). POP can provide such a school-wide learning structure.

Frontloading Common Core Knowledge

There are many options for frontloading the knowledge of Common Core. These range from online courses, to professional consultants coming in to help. Prepackaged programs written by "experts" can be purchased at a hefty price. Regardless of the choice made by districts, schools need ongoing support and time to practice to get this right. Instructing at this level will not be attained with a "sit-and-get" professional development model. The Common Core means that teachers must shift their practice and teach advanced materials to their students in more successful ways. How can we accomplish such a substantial change in classroom instruction in thousands of schools and tens of thousands of classrooms, and with millions of students with differing abilities, interests, and life goals? (Phillips & Hughes, 2012.) This is where POP comes in. POP is the perfect process for navigating the instructional shifts required to successfully implement the Common Core:

> Adopting the Common Core extends the teacher's role as coach, carefully designing activities to build specific skills, providing constructive feedback, and continually modifying lessons based on student understanding. Through professional development, teachers

learn how to assess and give meaningful, consistent feedback; to share what works with their peers; and adjust lessons appropriately.

(Phillips & Hughes, 2012)

Focus on Questioning Techniques

One such focus for schools to begin with in terms of POP and the Common Core is to examine questioning techniques. Teaching children to think at a higher level will require an astute understanding in the line of questioning that teachers offer students. No longer can teachers utilize low depth of knowledge (DOK) questions and elicit the types of response that the Common Core demands. Perhaps it might be worth investing in time to observe the questioning practices that are taking place within the classrooms of your buildings.

As teachers, we have to work on not only asking better questions but also asking questions better. And we have to be figuring out how to teach the students to do the same two things. Both of these include planning:

- How can we make better use of hinge-point questions to help us know what students need to move on in their learning?

- What question will I ask in the lesson to provide scaffolding to support the higher expectations?

- How do we want students to demonstrate their learning at high levels? This requires that we are familiar with the "critical words" we use to ask students to demonstrate their learning, whether on an assessment or in class conversation.

- What strategies will we use to increase student engagement, to involve all students in responding to the questions not just to the teacher but among themselves as well, to push their thinking higher (or deeper)?

(Dyer, 2013)

Principal Rob Stephenson of Farnsley Middle School in Louisville, KY, analyzes classroom questioning as an indicator of rigor and has adapted a quick observation tool to look specifically at the rigor of the verbs teachers use in questioning and task design (see Table 6.1).

This is a great checklist to use with POP to collect data about the kinds of questions that are being asked in your classrooms. At the end of the observation

Table 6.1 Rigor of verbs used in questioning and task design

Date	Period	Subject	Teacher
	Tally of questions asked (verb used?)	**Students' responses**	**Teacher answers (probing?)**
Knowledge & comprehension (DOK 1) *Define Restate* *List Identify* *Label Describe* *Recall Explain* *Memorize*		(Did students answer the questions or did the teacher give up and answer it herself?)	(Did the teacher answer her own question or did she probe for greater depth?)
Application & analysis (DOK 2) *Solve Classify* *Translate Compare* *Interpret Criticize* *Apply Categorize* *Use Distinguish*			
Synthesis & evaluation (DOK 3) *Estimate Invent* *Formulate Create* *Hypothesize Infer* *Appraise Predict* *Design Editorialize* *Dispute*			

time, a quick look at the range of verbs used indicates the degree to which the learning was pushed toward higher order thinking (look at Table 6.1 again). This plays out in the classroom in terms of the way student work is structured. Here is a look at how our expectations for deeper student learning could appear to an observer as the instruction moves through the levels:

- Students receive and are expected to *recall* and *remember* facts, rules, definitions, or information. The teachers, or just a few students, do most of the talking and the thinking, and tasks involve exact replication of directly stated material. Most students typically listen, copy notes, practice basic skills, and answer questions with "single-word" answers. Students may or may not understand purpose, relevance, or connection with previous learning, their lives, or the world at large.

- Students use acquired knowledge to *solve problems, design solutions,* and complete work using very methodical methods that require little elaboration. While the work and expectations require limited cognitive demand for completion, the work is interesting, compelling, and somewhat purposeful for students.

- Students *demonstrate their understanding of key concepts through quality classroom conversation;* thought-provoking writing prompts; and engaging, intricate tasks. Students are required to engage with the conceptual ideas that underlie their procedures in order to successfully complete a task and develop understanding. However, there is limited connection to real-world applications.

You could use this tally tool developed by Williamson and Blackburn to chart your observations about questioning techniques and talk with teachers about questions in class (Williamson & Blackburn, n.d.) (see Table 6.2).

Students competently *think in sophisticated ways to synthesize* information; evaluate context; and apply their knowledge and skills to solve real-word, perplexing, and unfamiliar problems. Instructors build a community of learners in the classroom who advance one another to *construct meaning of key concepts, complex dilemmas,* and *compelling issues* (Williamson & Blackburn, n.d.). There are so many instructional components to the Common Core that beginning with questioning techniques as a focus would render a big bang for your buck.

Table 6.2 Charting observations about questioning techniques

Questions asked by teacher	
Low-level/rote questions	High-level/application questions
Teacher response to student answers	
Low-level student responses accepted	High-level responses accepted or probing/extended questions asked

The Use of Graphic Organizers

Another possible focus to use to begin the professional development for teachers' implementation of the Common Core could be the use of graphic organizers for students to display their thinking. Graphic organizers help create visual displays for students to structure their thinking. This is particularly effective with English language learners. Kaufman and Wandberg (2010) list the use of graphic organizers as one of the most powerful instructional strategies a teacher can utilize. McLaughlin and Overturf (2013) state:

> It is essential that we use explicit instruction when teaching our students to use the graphic organizers:
>
> 1. First, we explain how the organizer works.
> 2. Next, we demonstrate how to use it.
> 3. Then we engage students in guided practice.
> 4. After that, students practice on their own.
> 5. Finally, we engage our students in reflection about how to use the organizer and what they have learned. (McLaughlin & Overturf, 2013)

I asked for this!

These visual representations assist the student in organizing abstract "big picture" information that is new, overwhelming or misunderstood in the new standards. Research supports the utilization of graphic organizers as a contributing factor in improving student performance (http://www.livebinders.com/play/play/297779).

Teaching Critical Vocabulary Needed for the Common Core

Finally, you might begin with a focus on vocabulary used in instruction. Pay close attention to the academic vocabulary that students will be required to know and use on standardized assessments for the Common Core State Standards. How are these critical nouns and verbs being taught to mastery as children move up the grade levels? Perhaps teachers might need some frontloading of professional development on how to best teach vocabulary? Marilee Sprenger (2013) offers 11 tips for effective teaching of the vocabulary required by the Common Core:

1 Introduce a word and determine a definition or description with your students. Using their own language to describe what a word means will help students remember the appropriate definition.

2 Have students draw a picture of the word or what the word represents. *Analyze*, for example, means to break something into its component parts. I have seen students' drawings that depict a figure breaking a stick over its knees, block towers tumbling down, and unpacked Russian nesting dolls.

3 Ask students to find synonyms and antonyms for each word on a list. Synonyms are often used as definitions, so the process of finding and discussing these terms is crucial. Give each student a nametag that includes either the critical word or its synonym. Let students figure out which words are related and form synonym circles. The circles can line up together or work in groups that day.

4 To store words more easily in automatic memory, let students compose jingles or songs for words and definitions.

5 Have students create semantic maps or mind maps for some words.

6 Vocabulary gloves: Have students write the vocabulary word on the back of cheap canvas gloves. On the front, have them write a sentence on the palm, synonyms on the thumb, pointer, and middle finger, an antonym on the ring finger, and the definition on the pinky. Gloves can be used for independent or paired practice.

7 Have students act out word meanings to activate their procedural memory.

8 You and your students can create review games to reinforce the words. For example, here are some guidelines for "Vocabulary Bingo":

   - Hand out Bingo cards with definitions in the squares.
   - Students ask each other if they know what word fits one of the definitions and to sign the square if they know.
   - Once all squares have signatures, draw student names from a container; all students with that signature cover the square.
   - Students yell "Bingo!" when they have five in a row. The five students whose names are covered on the card must know the correct word.

9 Create vocabulary word pages in a notebook. When the word appears in different contexts or content areas, students can return to that page and add new information. This will help them use the words more easily in writing and speaking.

10 Model the use of the words in your classroom. The more often that students hear them, the more automatic their use of those words will become.

11 Be aware of eye-accessing cues. When a student is struggling with a test question, he or she will often be looking down, which accesses emotions— perhaps the emotion of feeling "dumb." To access information, such as definitions or visual memories of words, eyes must be looking up. When you observe this, stand over the student and ask a question that forces him or her to look up, possibly triggering the information. (Sprenger, 2013)

After frontloading of effective strategies for teaching critical vocabulary a checklist could be used to look for particular use of these strategies within classrooms. Components of such a checklist would include a word wall, nonlinguistic visual representations of such words displayed in the room, the repeated use of the vocabulary during instruction, use of the words in displayed content and language objectives, and plans written by the teacher to teach the words.

Using a Book Study to Disseminate Knowledge

At the dual language elementary school a large-scale book study on the Common Core was done over the course of a semester to frontload the instructional knowledge needed to use with POP. There is a plethora of books written on the subject. The school picked from a list supplied by the International Reading Association. Five different books were chosen that were written about the Common Core in areas focusing on early childhood to working with English language learners. Teachers self-selected the book that they chose to read and groups were formed. These groups were completely different in makeup from the POP groups already in place at the school. Possible book study models were presented and each group chose one accordingly. The groups were given the dates that they would be expected to meet along with a date for a final presentation to the faculty. They were off and running in their pursuit of knowledge regarding Common Core instructional best practices. Each group operated independently in terms of organization. At the end of the semester the faculty reconvened and each group presented the highlights and "aha" moments from their book. After the presentations, two teachers led the faculty in the creation of a check-list to use in POP for the second semester. This checklist was based on a selected few big ideas required from the Common Core. This list consisted of questioning techniques, using graphic organizers for students to frame their thinking, including cultural sensitivity within lessons, and upping the ante with vocabulary used with the students. This checklist would be the tool to use for "look fors" during the observations for POP for the second semester.

PARCC materials

Are You Ready?

What has your district/school done to prepare teachers to teach at the level of rigor required by the Common Core? An informal canvas of various teachers around the state reveals that not much, if anything, has been done formally. According to Bill and Melinda Gates's survey entitled, "Primary Sources 2012: America's Teachers on the Teaching Profession," a majority (78%) of teachers are aware of the Common Core State Standards, many do not yet feel "prepared to teach to these new standards" (Bill and Melinda Gates Foundation, 2012). This is frightening considering that in many states currently a percentage of teacher evaluations is tied to test scores. The new Common Core assessments coupled with little teacher preparation spell out disaster for all stakeholders.

Begin with a focus. Frontload the information and put POP in place to being the ongoing professional development needed to promote mastery of the instructional skills. Teachers need time to practice, reflect, and receive feedback. This process is no different than good teaching we would put in place with our students.

One final thought in terms of preparation for this new endeavor is in terms of resources. Perhaps you need to take inventory of the teaching resources you have at hand to use for Common Core implementation. Do you have enough nonfiction texts? Are your current textbooks written and aligned with the Common Core? Are you set up in terms of technology to give the assessment required and aligned to the CCSS?

School administrators need strong leadership skills to successfully implement the new standards. Pete Reed (2013) identifies these skills neces-sary to make instructional changes within an educational system:

- A shared vision and a laser-like focus on that vision.
- High-fidelity collaborative action directed by the vision.

- Organizational structures and standards of practice aligned with the vision.

- A corps of teachers who build individual and collective capacity to make the vision a reality.

To conclude, define a focus to begin with in this process. I would recommend a tightly developed choice of strategies. Devise a checklist to use in POP. Frontload the professional development needed whether it be through a book study or a professional consultant coming in to your school. Set the wheels in motion and let POP work its magic.

Four Years Into the Process

The function of leadership is to create leaders, not followers.

(Ralph Nader)

One year our Principal had to take a leave of absence beginning in November and lasting for the rest of the school year. Curiously enough, an interim Principal was not assigned. One of the Principals of a neighboring school would check in on us periodically to see if we needed anything. We didn't. In fact, our test scores were just as high that year as they had ever been. Discipline referrals remained steady and staff meetings were held led by the administrative assistant to tend to the business at hand. Remarkably, the school had a responsible staff capable of sustaining the building with or without him. This is the mark of good leadership.

Utilizing a Shared Model of Leadership

How do you go about setting up a shared model of leadership? Linda Lambert (2002) states, "Instead of looking to the Principal alone for instructional leadership, we need to develop leadership capacity among all members of the school community." She goes on to say:

> The old model of formal, one-person leadership leaves the substantial talents of teachers largely untapped. Improvements achieved under this model are not easily sustainable; when the principal leaves, promising programs often lose momentum and fade away. As a result of these and other weaknesses, the old model has not

met the fundamental challenge of providing quality learning for all students.

(Lambert, 2002)

Administrators come and go. Principal Barbara Kohm explains: "The more adept I became at solving problems, the weaker the school became" (Kohm, 2002). Is your staff dependent on you as the Principal to lead the way? Or have you engaged in a shared leadership model that empowers teachers to lead the school alongside of you? A shared leadership model of governance means Principals seek out others in their school to build partnerships, tap others' strengths, and jointly move the vision forward (Burgess & Bates, 2009). What practices will remain in place once you are gone? The old model of formal, one-person leadership leaves the substantial talents of teachers largely untapped (Lambert, 2002). This is a waste of expertise, skills, and knowledge from which all could benefit. As William D. Greenfield (2005) writes, "The challenge for a school leader is to spark and sustain a collaborative dialogue and to work with and *through* teachers to develop a shared commitment to implementing the desired practices effectively" (p. 249). School leaders engaging staff in professional conversations should strive for a set of operating norms that will help ensure interdependence is in play. An example of these norms might read as follows:

- All voices are heard.
- We operate by listening and asking probing questions.
- All faculty members are engaged in decision making, as appropriate.
- All faculty members know the goals we're working to achieve. (Burgess & Bates, 2009)

Don't get me wrong: Principals are needed at schools, no doubt. Principals are the heads of the ship, only the Principal cannot be the only rower. There are just not enough hours in a day for the Principal to accomplish all that is required of him any longer. Schools must utilize a shared model of leadership to truly rise above mediocrity.

A shared leadership model requires the Principal to "let go of overseeing everything." Some examples of what this might look like in our schools have included the following:

- Different teachers, based on their expertise, have taken over as providers of professional development ranging in topics that include formative vs summative assessment, expanding student engagement, second language acquisition best instructional strategies, and a balanced literacy approach.

- One teacher has taken over all of the data collection and organization of the school. Her love of data has been recognized and now the entire staff looks to her as the expert. She is!

- Another teacher has taken over to ramp up the level of literacy engagement in our school. Her creative ideas have led to a devotion to literacy for not only students but staff as well. We are beginning to see students develop a love of reading.

- We have several teachers from Spanish speaking countries at the dual language elementary school. They came up with the idea of offering a dance class for students to teach them the native dances of Mexico and the South American countries. The class takes place after school and it is overflowing with students. The teachers do this on their own volition with no remuneration.

- A kindergarten teacher now offers early morning yoga classes for teachers. "This class is a great way to begin the day and we enjoy being together learning yoga."

- One of our ELA teachers asked if she could form a team to assess the quality of our dual language program. We asked for volunteers and a committee was created. The ELA teacher oversees this committee. This is invaluable to me, as the administrator, for she has more expertise in this area than I do. I can count on her to ensure that we are implementing a first-rate program.

- Two teachers researched different models for summer school and asked if we could try a truly out of the box approach. They presented multiple sources of research to support the model and offered to organize the program. Using a pre- and post-assessment, the new model was deemed a huge success and one that will be used moving forward.

These are just a few of the many fruits being realized from operating within a shared leadership model. Do not be afraid to let go of some control. Embrace your teachers' talents and expertise. You might even see some teachers display some skills you did not know about.

Changes in Teacher Roles

Four years into the practice of POP has seen it morph into a design tailored by the staffs to meet their needs to get the job done. Even within buildings individual teams have developed personalities all their own. Possibly one of the best outcomes of this practice is that everyone is valued for some particular expertise. Teachers go to one another for help with everything from classroom management to data analysis. We have seen teachers begin to find research on their own and send it out to the staff for all to read. The teachers feel empowered as experts within not only their building, but as professionals.

The International Baccalaureate Coordinator holds weekly grade level team meetings in the elementary school. She noticed that since the implementation of POP grade level team meetings are more open and communication is stronger than it has ever been. Teachers are willing to share their ideas and thoughts for they know they will be honored and probably utilized. The teachers have learned how to give and receive feedback therefore, the communication is open and constructive, not just at the POP sessions, but in all aspects of work. Teachers have stepped up and not only designed structures but implemented them as well. Two valuable ideas have turned into realities at the elementary school. One is a mentoring program where all teachers that do not teach full time in the classrooms have taken on three or four at risk children as mentees. Mentors meet weekly with their mentees to provide adult support. Another idea by the same teacher was to host a "Career Day" at the elementary school. Truly by unlocking the creative and shared leadership potential by POP have multiple ideas come to fruition by staff members.

Immediate Return

POP is still relatively new at the inner city middle school. It has seen tremendous progression, however. At the start, teachers met after school every other week. Only 25 minutes were allotted for the conversations. Many times, however, teachers would stay and continue their conversations long after their contracted day had ended. After only one semester, however, school leadership was able to witness the changes occurring at the school. Because of that, weekly time was then granted for the groups during early-release PLC times. POP was validated through the granting of more time on a weekly basis. The POP groups also recognized how their conversations would be connected to weekly discussions centered around student data. The form the groups used at the start was modified to reflect more specific school and PLC goals. Teachers were now looking at backwards design and evidence seen in the classroom on a daily basis. There was also an increased emphasis on academic rigor, in conjunction with the transition into the Common Core. Teachers had the opportunity to fine-tune lessons with a purpose. The symbiotic relationship between the school's PLC and its POP groups should continue to lead to better teaching, more focused collaboration, and, bottom line, increased student achievement.

Metamorphosis

In the beginning stages of POP there was a strong dependence on a checklist to use during the observations. Teachers used the checklists to look for certain practices within the instruction. You can find several examples of checklists in the Appendices. After the first year, the checklists were not even used as the staff members knew what to look for. They had a clear understanding of the requirements of the particular focus of the school. The high school learned to implement the "Gradual Release of Responsibility Instructional Model" with fidelity. The elementary school became very competent at using instructional strategies that resulted in a more rapid acquisition of the second language. After two years in each school, these strategies would be given to new teachers as part of a mentoring and coaching model. In periodic professional learning communities they would be revisited as a spiral review for all but no longer was a checklist used as team members observed each other.

Solid Understandings

POP is a purely supportive framework that does not engage in evaluation in any form. Perhaps that is how the trust is able to develop so cohesively.

This process is independent totally of the Principal. Conversations are never shared outside the teams and feedback is given in a manner that is effective. With the teams being never more than eight in number, each teacher is observed once a semester. Over the course of the four years we have found that teams no larger than eight are ideal. With this size, each person gets observed once per semester. Obviously the smaller your teams, the more often teachers can get observed. This is certainly flexible in terms of organization. The strength of the process is that everyone benefits regardless of who is being observed. An observing teacher is always evaluating his own performance against what he is observing thinking in terms of how he might do something better within his own classroom. There is a true metacognition in regards to one's own teaching practices that is refined with the reflective feedback sessions done biweekly:

> For decades, educators have understood that we are all responsible for student learning. More recently, educators have come to realize that we are responsible for our own learning as well. But we usually do not move our eyes around the room—across the table—and say to ourselves, "I am also responsible for the learning of my colleagues."
>
> (Lambert, 2002)

Synergy

With the Common Core State Standards being adopted by the majority of states it is incumbent upon every administrator to provide high-quality professional development to ensure that teachers are prepared to teach at this level of rigor. As described in Chapter 6, we have since moved to using POP to implement the instructional changes necessary to implement the Common Core. This synergy distributes the load, provides support, and offers opportunities for practice within teachers' everyday jobs.

Synergy is defined as the interaction of multiple elements in a system to produce an effect different from or greater than the sum of their individual effects. The term *synergy* comes from the Greek word *synergia* συνέργια from *synergos*, συνεργός, meaning "working together." Geese use synergy while flying long distances. So, what can we learn from geese in terms of teamwork and collaboration?

- It is interesting to note that when geese fly in the V formation, they are able to increase their flying range by 71%. People who share a common direction and sense of community can get to where they are going more quickly and easily because they are traveling on the thrust of one another. POP's foundation is based on the goal and vision of the school (theleadership. wordpress.com/2006/ 06/10/synergy-why-do-geese-fly-in-a-v-formation/).

- Whenever a goose falls out of formation, it suddenly feels the drag and resistance of trying to go it alone and quickly gets back into formation to take advantage of the lifting power of the bird immediately in front. In POP teachers feel a sense of community, that they are part of a team working together to improve instructional practices that truly make a difference for children. Teachers need each other to dissect and discuss the new strategies required for the Common Core. This work is too hard to go it alone.

- The geese in the back of the V honk to encourage the members toward the front of the V. POP teams provide validation of practices done well. Encouragement is given through feedback and all members benefit from the conversations.

- Geese take turns leading the V formation. In POP leadership is shared and individuals take turns stepping up depending on the need for various skill sets or expertise. When a team is functioning well, various members of the team may take on the leadership role at different times. Everyone has the opportunity to serve in both the capacity of leader as well as follower (Wilson, 2012)

- Finally, when a goose gets sick, or is wounded by gunshot, and falls out, two geese fall out of formation and follow him down to help and protect him. They stay with him until he is either able to fly or until he is dead, and then they launch out on their own or with another formation until they catch up with their own group. When teachers struggle with various aspects of their own instruction team members discuss, model, and help the teacher make the needed changes. Articles are shared and support is given freely and generously until the teacher feels like he is having success in the classroom once again.

Next Steps for POP

Some next steps that have evolved for POP include the use of technology. Some teams have introduced the idea of using videos of the teachers being observed as tools to further enhance the conversations. Using a video helps when teachers are unable to get in to observe. If a teacher is absent on the POP session day, the teacher is expected to submit ideas, questions, and observations to the team lead to be shared with the team. Perhaps the session can be recorded so that the absent teacher can access the discussion at a later date. One teacher had the idea of compiling a collection of best instructional practices into a video for new teachers to view.

Speaking of new teachers, how do you bring new teachers up to speed rapidly? No one has years to wait for the novice teacher to become solid. POP accelerates the learning curve for new teachers as they get to see many lessons modeled and implemented. The elementary school routinely hires Spanish teachers from Spain, Columbia, and Mexico. POP has been instrumental in not only helping these new teachers get on board but also it has provided them with a vehicle for fostering relationships and having a network of support instantly.

Further Implications and Recommendations

Recommendations for future implementations of a Peer Observation Process should center on the organization and logistics of the processes within the building. To sum up steps needed for a successful implementation would include the following: Administrative support is vital, not only in the beginning stages, but continually throughout the process. Establishing a scheduled time for teachers to not only meet consistently, but to observe each other, is paramount to the success of the program. Possibly from time to time there might be a need to cover for teachers so that they can get in to do their observations. Would you have the time to cover? Is there a scheduled PLC time to utilize? If not, perhaps meeting before or after school might suffice. I often leave it up to my teams as to when to schedule a meeting if we find that our regular Monday afternoon gets taken over by something else. The options are before or after school and I leave it up to each team. Observations can last anywhere from 30 minutes to an hour. It is important to mobilize master teachers within the building to lead the instructional observation teams. The team leads need to be teachers that are respected within the building as high-quality teachers. They must have facilitating skills and be willing to take on the responsibility for the success of the teams. Frontloading of professional development for the leaders is necessary to aid them in the successful delivery of the academic discussions. It is helpful to establish some kind of accountability system to ensure that everyone is participating. Encourage team leads to let you know if there is a problem with participation. To be realistic we do understand that there are times when not everyone can get in to observe. We realize this but all teachers are expected to participate and engage in thoughtful conversation and dialogue in the feedback sessions. A thoughtful rollout of the process to the staff is required to garner buy-in. Schools should have a definite focus on which to concentrate the observations. This focus would align with the goals and objectives of the school. Putting into place some kind of data collection process to measure the success of the program would help determine the effectiveness. A recommendation would be to include multiple data points to increase the validity of the success measures. Finally, a recommendation would be made to meet quarterly with the team leaders to gather input as to the implementation success and make adjustments as needed. Identify any barriers that are in place for a successful implementation and problem solve ways to remove them.

What's Not to Love?

With four years into the process we have seen gains in so many areas for all of the schools described in this book. Student achievement has increased along with collaboration and collegiality. Teacher creativity and leadership has grown exponentially thus creating more job satisfaction. Teachers feel not only valued but trusted as the experts within their building and finally POP has provided for sustainability of practices that is not dependent on the administrator. Each year it is helpful to review not only the process but the rationale behind the process. You, as the administrator, need to share the data garnered from the focus thus recreating the buy-in. Use POP as a tool for instructional success and write it in your unified school improvement plan. Having it written in such a plan reiterates the nonnegotiability of the process and gives the message of the importance for *all teachers' participation*. Celebrate the successes and reload for the year. Remind the staff of the positive outcomes that result from teachers observing, reflecting, and practicing solid instructional strategies within the safety of POP.

In the four years during which this process has been used, our schools have won the Governor's Distinguished Award for Academic Growth in

Student Achievement in the state of Colorado every year. After two years at the high school, average yearly progress (AYP) was made for the first time ever. Increases in second language acquisition, as evidenced by the WIDA assessment, were made for elementary students. Both the high school and the elementary school rose to the top tier for evaluation from the state according to the School Performance Frameworks. (The middle school is still in its first year.) Besides these academic gains, cultural gains in collegiality have been realized as well. Turnover is low and morale is high. The teachers feel pride in their work and ownership of their schools. As a Principal, I would not want to ever oversee a school without this process in place. To conclude, POP is not the answer, but the process in which to find the answers that will make positive changes within your building.

Personal Stories of POP's Influence

There is nothing more satisfying than seeing hordes of people engaged to do good together because of the leadership you helped produce.

(Michael Fullan)

There are many similar reactions to the POP and its implementation in the various schools. "Where will we find the time to get into other classrooms?" "What if the observation turns into a judgment?" "We already have too many meetings after school, how can we find time for more?" To be fair, many teachers are also excited about having the opportunity to see what is going on in their peers' classes. This curiosity, however, would need to be valuable if it is to continue.

What many teachers find almost immediately is that this is more than simply watching someone teach. The time spent in the rooms turns into opportunities for reflection, for critique, for inspiration. The beauty of the program is how it impacts both the teacher being observed and the one observing. As talked about before, the bidirectional learning is one of its main strengths. The buy-in becomes almost immediate after just one cycle.

The following are stories from teachers and administrators who have participated in the POP for the last several years. All schools mentioned earlier in the book are represented in these stories.

Mike

I had been teaching for 10 years when this program was introduced at the high school. We, as a school, were on the hot seat as far as test scores and necessary improvement. The district mandate was that administration had to be in every room every day, and we knew that that wasn't realistic. This program came as a result of discussions around how we could improve as a school.

Because I was on our Building Leadership Team, I was assigned a Peer Observation group. There were a handful of groups, each with about six teachers and paraprofessionals. Mine was made up of teachers who had been in the field for over 20 years, on down to a first-year teacher. I would be the first teacher to be observed.

I was honestly nervous about having so many teachers come into my room and watch my teaching. I felt confident in my abilities, but I will admit that I had gotten comfortable with those abilities. What happened, I can say with certainty, was that my teaching changed. I was able to see my teaching through the eyes of my peers. They were validating some of the techniques that I used, but more importantly, they were challenging every move I made. I was forced to think about every lesson, whether I was being observed that day or not.

I'll never forget one piece of feedback that the brand new teacher gave me. She simply commented about the tone of voice I used with some of my students. What I saw as a harmless way of responding was shown to me to be somewhat mean. On hearing that, I felt horrible. But I didn't feel like she had said anything wrong. What she did was force me to rethink how I spoke to all of my students. I was reminded of how powerful my words and my tone were. It actually shook me a bit. That conversation was over four years ago and I think about it every day. That's the power of POP.

I've also been fortunate to see some amazing teaching. I was blown away when I went into an advanced Spanish class at the school. The teacher was experienced not only with the language but with good teaching. I don't think I stopped smiling the entire class. Although I couldn't understand more than a few words, I was able to observe *good teaching*. I saw how powerful having a rapport with students could be. Again, it's been over four years and I still tell people about my observations of her class.

I'm now involved with the POP at another school after a two-year hiatus. Again, it is amazing how invigorating it is to my teaching. I've had invaluable feedback from peers, in a way that empowers both them and me. I also see how it can have such a powerful impact on new teachers. Throughout the years, I've been able to really strengthen the feedback that I give to my peers. I'm much more confident when I walk into a classroom; I feel that I can critique any part of a lesson that the teacher wishes. This process is not only improving my teaching, it's making me a stronger teacher–leader as well.

Erin

It was my first job ever. My assignment was to teach art at two different schools, the middle and the high school. I was in a brand new place surrounded by people I did not really know. I had done my student teaching; one placement was really good, the other, not so much.

Immediately I was placed on a Peer Observation team. We began the rotations and I began to watch others in my group. The process was truly helpful as I was able to observe teachers of all content areas. I quickly noticed what worked and what didn't.

Meanwhile I felt like I was drowning in my middle school classes. I quickly volunteered to be observed so that I could get some much needed feedback as to how to get these classes under control. The middle school students were running the show and I felt helpless. I conveyed this to my team and asked for help.

My team lead came over and immediately recognized issues that needed to be fixed. He told me that I needed to gain control the minute the students walked in the door and that I should begin each class with a warm-up. This warm-up would set the tone for the class from the very beginning. I put that into place the next day and did it ever make a difference! I call my warm-ups the "do nows" and I still have them in place today, four years later.

Another aspect that I came to really appreciate from participating in this process was the chance to practice giving and receiving feedback. I have found that, as a teacher working with students, this skill is so important. When do teachers get a chance to practice this very valuable skill? I learned through this process how important it is to operate from a strength model, focusing on what is working well, instead of what is not working. Conversely, it is also important to address instructional and classroom management issues in an honest and helpful manner. We were a team helping each other. There was no judgment or evaluation. My group became very valuable to me, in terms of support and collegiality. This was very important, as I was so new to the profession.

Working with veteran teachers in this process shaped me as the teacher that I am today. Being able to observe all of these amazing teachers helped me to pick and choose the aspects that I wanted to incorporate into my daily routines and instructional strategies. With new administrators we no longer have this process but I wish that we did as it helps us to continually grow in our craft. Possibly more importantly, it creates teams of trusted peers who help each other navigate this complex job of teaching.

Paul

I was a part of the POP in its early years. I was a first- and second-year teacher. I eventually moved into a staff leadership position; I led my own group. I learned a lot of good lessons from this, particularly as a new teacher.

I think the first thing is really having those difficult conversations. Naturally, when you start this process at your schools, as we were doing, it's surface-level conversations, very superficial. People are very congratulatory; you're just trying to build that trust in the group. But inevitably you're going to have those situations where you will have to give some difficult feedback. I had that situation.

What was really interesting about it was that I was a new teacher, and the particular staff member had been teaching for eight to nine years. But really, we were able to establish the professionalism between the two of us. We sat down together in an individual manner; this was not in front of the group. We were then able to have a conversation about what we *both* saw. I wasn't telling him anything that he wasn't already aware of. But it was the ability to process what actually happened, and not just concentrate on what were necessarily the challenges presented in that particular class, but how do we move forward to make things better.

The real lessons were that these difficult conversations were important because it holds up the fidelity of the program. Also that it's professionalism—we don't want to do something that's not effective. If we can't get past some of the superficial things and get to the point where we're really addressing the challenges in classrooms, then it's not working. I, as a new teacher, felt really good about being a part of that. I recognized that these things don't happen right away; some trust in the group has to be there. I think that's a natural process, and I'm glad I was able to experience that firsthand.

Stacy

I'm the Spanish teacher at the high school. I'm also the only language teacher so I'm the department. That can be kind of isolating. I don't necessarily feel like I have a "team" that's a good fit for me. When we started doing POP, I really looked forward to going into the language arts classes because I felt like I had more in common with those teachers. We had more of a background to share with one another.

It was time to go into one teacher's language arts classroom. I went in and I sat in the back. I was watching her do her instruction. She was asking questions of the class. I noticed that when she would ask a question, one boy would raise his hand and everyone else would just very quietly sit there. And every time she asked a question, that same boy would raise his hand, and she kept calling on him and calling on him. At that very moment, I realized that *that was me*, especially in my native Spanish class where the students already know so much Spanish so they didn't have to function so much by learning the language, but by learning the grammar.

So I had a big epiphany that her instruction was *my instruction*. When I left her classroom, we did talk about the fact that I had noticed that about her and about myself. What I did was get these Glad-Ware containers. I put the names of every student on a little slip of paper. I then put the names inside the containers and labeled one for each class. Now, if I'm ever asking a question, I pull out a student's name, I say the name, and then I ask the question. It gives the student some thinking time, some lead-in time. It really made a difference. I was so grateful for the epiphany moment that I had from the POP.

Kira

I'm a Peer Observation team leader at the elementary school. I've been so interested in watching how the groups' dynamics have changed from the first year that we met together to the second year. The first year I think we were really trying to figure out what our conversations were about. We were good about giving lots of compliments, saying the things that we saw that were really working well in the class, and starting to have some questions for each other. By the second year, the conversation really naturally, and easily, moved into compliments but also, "So tell me more about this." "Why were you doing this piece?" "I love that idea I want to use it in my classroom." It was interesting to see the conversations move to a sort of philosophical level in terms of asking why we were doing what we're doing, how we were doing what we're doing, are the things that we're doing in our classroom really matching with what we believe about education and best practice and dual language. We had a lot of those conversations this year, and that we really exciting to me.

I found a lot of encouragement from the group to think about what I was doing in my own classroom. Also, to think really flexibly about how to use time, to think about the things that needed to be accomplished and take lots of ideas from other partners in this group. I got to think really creatively about how to get done what really needed to be done in the best way possible.

It's also been really fun to just see the group evolve and mature. Each group seems to have its own personality. Our group really grew into a trusting group that was willing to ask questions and really think about things. I didn't feel like we needed to challenge each other in a way that ended up feeling defensive, but there was a lot of deep thinking about what we're doing and why we're doing it.

Carolina

I am from Spain but I have been teaching here in the United States for four years. Teaching in Spain is very different than teaching here in the US. In Spain, I taught music and special education. I was also a coteacher for all subject areas in first and second grades. Here, I teach kindergarten. After my first year the district implemented a new reading program. We were given a book to read to get us started. Being able to go in and see my peers implement this new reading initiative was extremely valuable, particularly in the area of literacy centers. Once I saw how my teammate had her centers set up it made perfect sense for me. I immediately made the changes in my room to mirror my teammates.

Another aspect of Peer Observation that has been so very helpful is to see both teachers and children in other grades. It helps for me to visit first grade as I have a keen understanding of where my children need to be in order to be successful on day one as they graduate to the next level. It is really nice to watch my former students and see them be so successful as they move up through the grades. Finally, it is nice to see not only other grades, but other content areas as well such as music and art. I feel that I have a thorough understanding of the school in which I teach.

Cara

I have been teaching for 10 years so I would consider myself a veteran teacher, someone not new to the business. I like my class to be very organized and I run a tight ship, if you will. I am also very particular about my classroom management.

I am the leader of my Peer Observation group. We had just changed teams so I was excited to observe some teachers that I had not seen before. I was scheduled to go and observe Michelle, a first grade teacher. What I observed was "jaw dropping!"

Michelle's students entered the room and knew exactly where to go and what to do. It was very apparent that she was the instructional leader and they were the learners. She used colorful plastic cups filled with letters for her phonics lessons. Each cup was numbered to match the material that belonged to it. That way if materials got misplaced they could readily be put back in place by matching number to number. The children got their cups and plastic bags and went to work.

I left school that day and drove straight to Target. I bought colorful cups and other supplies to organize my room just like Michelle had done. I had the materials in place by the next day and the results were immediate! My phonics instruction changed from that very day as a result of Michelle's observation. I had one student go from knowing one letter and sound to knowing 10, all in the course of one week. I feel like a big piece was my new-found organization. Truly through revamping simple guided instruction did I realize stronger results in phonics.

Dani

One of the biggest concerns I had entering the process was how I was going to add one more thing to my plate, which was already full. As a first-year teacher, I was feeling pretty overwhelmed from the start.

I have gained a lot of great ideas to incorporate into my own class-room after watching other, more experienced teachers interact with our kids. I realized that I was forcing silence on my kids too frequently (and get-ting unreasonably upset when, as middle schoolers, they could not meet my unreasonable expectations). I began to think critically about when and why I was expecting independent work, and have since provided them with more opportunities to interact with partners and chat. This has dramatically improved the atmosphere in my classroom.

I have also found awesome solutions to small problems, like how to use a PowerPoint without losing engagement every time I have to change a slide or how to do attendance without distracting my kids from their warm-up.

I have also had the good fortune to observe one of the teachers in my grade level team. Seeing what my kids succeeded at in that class gave me an idea of what note formats they were used to and allowed me to incorporate these familiar procedures into my own classes so that I could reduce instruction time.

I really appreciate this opportunity to improve my teaching. I doubt that I would have taken the time to get into another classroom every few weeks if it wasn't for POP because of the amount of other work that is on my plate right now. However, the time put in has paid off exponentially in my classroom. Other teachers have been in my position and are my number one resource on my path to becoming a successful educator!

Michael

As the process got started, my primary concern was that teachers might feel threatened by exposing their weaknesses to their colleagues. Since teachers are not usually trained evaluators or coaches, there is also the potential for teachers to focus on negative aspects of the lesson, rather than the positives and focusing on one to two questions or areas for improvement. Another concern related to whether faculty would honor the Peer Observation schedule.

As an experienced, veteran teacher in a Peer Observation group with a first-year teacher as well as experts in their content areas, I am gaining insights that are helping to refine my teaching. From our conversations, I have learned that the more micromanagement-based aspects of instruction are an area for improvement. As a result, I am more cognizant and intentional with my planning around the logistical components of my lesson. This includes more frontloading of vocabulary, precision partnering, and more efficiently managing time.

I hope that we continue to become increasingly confident with opening our classroom doors to guests. Moreover, I envision an environment where we feel safer questioning the practices of one another, remembering that our purpose is to improve instructional practices for the sake of student learning. The Peer Observation Process has the potential for teachers to display massive growth. I especially like being partnered with teachers across grade levels, content areas, and years of experience or mastery.

Amy

I think the POP Process has had a very positive impact on the school as a whole. Perhaps one of the most important pieces it seems to have brought is a culture of teachers as learners, in which they have open discussions around their own practice. It seems that teachers are excited to discuss instruction with each other and enjoy the opportunity to be in each other's rooms, learning with one another. What is interesting to me is that because we have worked to honor the wishes of teachers for the POP program to be teacher driven, I can't exactly say how much teachers discuss and challenge each other in these conversations. I think the POP program has worked well with other systems and expectations that have been put into place to help school culture, climate, and moral overall, but without being an actual part of the conversation I don't feel that I'm much of the expert in the exact impact they've had. Ultimately, I think this statement in itself is a positive part of the program, as it is truly teacher led and driven.

I also noticed something else as we did our learning walks. When we first started learning walks last year there was a lot of trepidation from teachers around why we would be in each other's classrooms, concerns around teachers evaluating or judging one another, etc. Now there is a lot of enthusiasm and appreciation for the process, with teachers appreciating the opportunity to see the instruction and learning going on in each other's classrooms. I think the experience with POP has allowed teachers to truly develop as a learning community and see each other as instructional partners rather than "competition," for lack of a better word. Instead of feeling concern at being in classrooms outside of their own POP groups, they were excited to see some of the other instruction happening in the building.

Kristina

At the start of the program, I was concerned that it would be difficult to give veteran teachers feedback. It is a bit intimidating coming in as a first year and giving feedback on specific focus areas to your coworkers who have been mastering the craft of teaching for years.

Even though I was nervous, I do believe that this program has helped to make me a better teacher. I have seen results in the feedback I have received, along with picking up awesome techniques and routines from other classrooms. It is extremely helpful as a first year to know what is going on in other rooms. I feel much more confident.

As this program continues throughout the year, I hope to make progress from the suggestions I have received. I hope to constantly improve after every cycle, whether it is a cycle where I am being observed or a cycle where I am observing someone else. I also see the Peer Observations as a great opportunity to build respect, community and trust within the school staff.

Peter

Although I was pretty positive about the initial implementation of POP, I was concerned about more meeting time after school. At the school, we had a Peer Observation Process a couple of years ago that got started. It died out, though, because there was no organization of follow-through. After the first few afterschool sessions I realized that these weren't meetings, however, but opportunities for teachers to talk about instructional strategies, share feedback, and truly collaborate, not a waste of time in any way.

The results have been immediate. So far I would say I feel less isolated, knowing that my peers might be along for a class period and that I will receive some valued, nonjudgmental feedback. Also, it's been great to visit some other teachers and see their skill, enthusiasm and variety of teaching practices. This has encouraged me to try some new techniques and think critically about my own practices.

Ian

As a Principal, it is at times hard to determine what professional development projects are the most worthwhile to implement and at what expense to the cumulative school calendar of PD. When one of our teachers approached us last year about creating a Peer Observation Process (POP), we were excited, but a bit guarded for a handful of reasons. We wanted authentic feedback and valuable feedback, so inherently we had reservations about how impactful peer-on-peer analysis would be and we asked a good deal of questions. (i.e., When would it occur? Would it take the place of other PD opportunities? Did it align with our school vision of creating a culture of rigor/higher expectations for all? Was the feedback given going to be valuable and how would novice educators truly be able to contribute from an observational standpoint? And ultimately, who would run it and oversee the progress?) As an administrator, sometimes it is hard to release the reins, especially if there are any doubts surrounding the current pedagogy occurring in the school. We felt comfortable with the balance of ability levels of our staff and wanted a nice balance for our groupings, and once we felt confident in the above criteria being met, we opted to let the teachers run with it.

When the program was initially proposed, we sat down and brainstormed with him what it would look like. He asked for an extra plan period to organize and implement its inception. We liked the idea of a culture of feedback that was non-evaluative but more of a support network for one another. We wanted to maintain a focus on our UIP action steps of intentional planning and first best instruction with a major emphasis on rigor and higher order thinking. We agreed that there needed to be some guidance on how teachers worked with one another and shared their feedback with one another, but we were on board with the idea. We needed buy-in from the staff in order for it to work and we wanted complete participation. Our confidence in Mr. Lamond's ability to motivate his peers and to make it come to fruition was essential.

Mr. Lamond organized an after-school meeting, shared his vision, and asked teachers for their input. We had 100% participation from all teachers and the program took off. Initially, it was done as a strictly voluntary biweekly meeting in which the staff congregated for 30 minutes after school on Wednesdays to debrief their observations of the selected teacher. It has grown into a 30-minute session that we now incorporate into our data team meetings. The level of trust the program has created among staff members, the collegiality, and the improvement of pedagogy are all evident. It has been a remarkable program and has begun to trickle down into other schools in our district.

The impact this program brings to a staff is so powerful. We see example after example from teachers who have been using this in their schools illustrating the true benefits of teachers working together. Accolades aside, teachers become better at what they do. The school climate and culture improve to the point where new identities are created. This was seen in all three schools mentioned throughout this book. This is not a coincidence.

First-year teachers who normally will spend an entire year, if not more, getting acclimated into their positions are now receiving the support for a cadre of peers to speed up the learning process. Experienced teachers are able to critically reflect on their philosophy and continue to model what it means to be a lifelong learner. Administrators are no longer seen as the only instructional experts in the building. In fact, they realize that they are surrounded by experts, and these experts are being empowered to demonstrate their abilities. And the biggest beneficiaries of this program? The students. Again, it is no coincidence that in each building in which POP was implemented, scores soared.

References

Ash, D., & Levitt, K. (2003). Working within the zone of proximal development: Formative assessment as professional development. *Journal of Science Teacher Education, 14*(1), 1–313.

Baron, D. (2008). Imagine: Professional development that changes practice. *Principal Leadership: High School Edition, 8,* 56–58.

Bill and Melinda Gates Foundation. (2012). Primary sources 2012: America's teachers on the teaching profession. Available at http://www.scholastic.com/primarysources/pdfs/Gates2012_full.pdf.

Bourne-Hayes, C. (2010). *Comparing novice and experienced teachers on perceptions about peer observation as professional development* (doctoral dissertation). Available at http://eric.ed.gov/?id=ED519873.

Bowers, D. (1999). *Teachers' use of peer observation and feedback as a means of professional development.* Unpublished doctoral dissertation. University of Southern California.

Brady, M. (2012). Eight problems with Common Core Standards. *Washington Post: The Answer Sheet by Valerie Strauss,* August 21, 2012. Available at http://www.washingtonpost.com/blogs/answer-sheet/post/eight-problems-with-common-core-standards/2012/08/21/821b300a-e4e7-11e1-8f62-58260e3940a0_blog.html.

Brown, J. (2012). Cost doesn't spell success for Colorado schools using consultants to improve achievement. Available at: http://www.denverpost.com/investigations/ci_19997418.

Buchanan, J., & Khamis, M. (1999). Teacher renewal, peer observations, and the pursuit of best practice. *Issues in Educational Research, 9*(1), 1–14.

Bullough, R. V., & Pinnegar, S. (2001). Guidelines for quality in autobiographical forms of self-study research. *Educational Researcher, 30*(3), 13–21.

Burgess, J., & Bates, D. (2009). *Other duties as assigned.* Alexandria, VA: ASCD.

Burke, K. (2000). Results-based professional development. *National Association of Secondary School Principals, 84,* 29–37.

Cain, J. H., & Smith, T. E. (2007). *The revised and expanded book of raccoon circles.* Dubuque, IA: Kendall/Hunt Publishing.

Calkins, L., Ehrenworth, M., & Lehman, C. (2012). *Pathways to the Common Core.* Portsmouth, NH: Heinemann.

Chance, P. L., & Segura, S. N. (2009). A rural high school's collaborative approach to school improvement. *Journal of Research in Rural Education, 24*(5), 1–12. available at http://jrre.vmhost.psu.edu/wp-content/uploads/2014/02/24-5.pdf.

City, E. A., Elmore, R. F., Fiarman, S. E., & Teitel, L. (2009). *Instructional rounds in education: A network approach to improving teaching and learning.* Cambridge, MA: Harvard Educational Press.

Cohen, J. (1988). *Statistical power analysis for the behavioral sciences* (2nd edn.). New York, NY: Academic Press.

Cosh, J. (1998). Peer observation in higher education. A reflective approach. *Innovations in Education and Training International, 35*(2), 171–176.

Dantonio, M. (2001). *Collegial coaching: inquiry into the teaching self* (2nd edn.). Bloomington, IN: Phi Delta Kappa International.

Darling-Hammond, L., & McLaughlin, M. W. (1995). Policies that support professional development in the era of reform. *Phi Delta Kappa, 76*(8), 597–604.

DeLong, T. J. (2011). Three questions for effective feedback. *Harvard Business Review.* Available at: http://blogs.hbr.org/2011/08/three-questions-for-effective-feedback/.

Desimone, L. M., Porter, A. C., Garet, M. S., Yoon, K. S., & Birman, B. F. (2002). Effects of professional development on teachers' instruction: Results from a three-year longitudinal study. *Educational Evaluation and Policy Analysis, 24*(2), 81–112. Available at http://outlier.uchicago.edu/computerscience/OS4CS/landscapestudy/resources/Desimone,Porter,%20Garet,%20Yoon,%20and%20Birman,%202002%20(1).pdf.

Desimone, L. M., Smith, T. M., & Ueno, K. (2006). Are teachers who need sustained, content-focused professional development getting it? An administrator's dilemma. *Educational Administration Quarterly, 42*(2), 179–215.

Dyer, K. (2013). Higher-order questions, rigor, and meeting the Common Core State Standards. Available at http://www.nwea.org/blog/2013/higher-order-questions-rigor-meeting-common-core-state-standards/.

Elliott, J. (2004). Using research to improve practice: The notion of evidence-based practice. In C. Day & J. Sachs (Eds.), *International handbook on the continuing professional development of teachers* (pp. 264–290). Maidenhead: Open University Press.

Eun, B. (2008). Making connections: Grounding professional development in the developmental theories of Vygotsky. *The Teacher Educator, 43*(2), 134–155.

Eun, B. (2010). A Vygotsky theory-based professional development: Implications for culturally diverse classrooms. *Professional development in education, 37*(3), 319–333. Abingdon: Taylor & Francis.

Frenkel, E., & Wu, H. H. (2013). Common Core standards for mathematics: The real issues. *Huffington Post*. Available at http://www.huffingtonpost.com/edward-frenkel-/common-core-standards-for_1_b_4079831.html.

Fullan, M. (1993). *Change forces: Probing the depths of educational reform.* New York, NY: Falmer.

Fullan, M., & Steigelbauer, S. (1991). *The new meaning of educational change* (2nd edn.). Toronto, ON: OISE Press.

Fullan, M. G. (1991). *The new meaning of educational change.* London: Cassell.

Garet, M., Porter, A., Desimone, L., Birman, B., & Yoon, K. S. (2001). What makes professional development effective? Results from a national sample of teachers. *American Educational Research Journal, 38*(4), 915–945.

Golden-Biddle, K. (2012). How to change an organization without blowing it up. *MIT Sloan Management Review, 54*(2). Available at http://sloanreview.mit.edu/article/how-to-change-an-organization-without-blowing-it-up/.

Gordon, S. P. (2004). *Professional development in education: Empowering learning communities.* New York, NY: Pearson Education.

Greenfield, W. (2005). Leading the teacher work group. In L. W. Hughes (Ed.), *Current issues in school leadership* (pp. 245–264). Mahwah, NJ: Erlbaum Associates.

Guskey, T. (1995). Professional development in education: In search for the optimal mix. In T. R. Guskey & M. Huberman (Eds.), *Professional development in education: New paradigms and practices* (pp. 114–132). New York, NY: Teachers College Press.

Guskey, T. (2000). *Evaluating professional development.* Thousand Oaks, CA: Corwin Press.

Halsey, V. (2011). *Brilliance by design: Creating learning experiences that connect, inspire, and engage.* San Francisco, CA: Berrett-Koehler Publishers, Inc.

Hammersley-Fletcher, L., & Orsmond, P. (2004). Evaluating our peers: Is peer observation a meaningful process? *Studies in Higher Education, 29*(4), 489–503.

Hammersley-Fletcher, L., & Orsmond, P. (2005). Reflecting on reflective practices within peer observation. *Studies in Higher Education, 30*(2), 213–224.

Hansen, S. D. (2010). Inviting observation. *Principal Leadership, 11*(2), 52–54, 56.

Harmon, H. L. (2001, March). *Attracting and retaining teachers in rural areas.* Paper presented at the meeting of the American Association of Colleges for Teacher Education, Dallas, TX.

Haslam, M. B., & Seremet, C. P. (2001). Strategies for improving professional development: A guide for school districts. Available at http://www.centerforcsri.org/research/improvement.cgi?st=s&sr=SR003540.

Hattie, J., & Timperley, H. (2007). The power of feedback. *Review of Educational Research, 77*(1), 81–112.

Hertzog, H. S. (1995). In-service education for staff development. In J. K. Lemlech (Ed.), *Becoming a professional leader* (pp. 141–171). New York, NY: Scholastic.

Hiebert, J., Gallimore, R., & Stigler, J. W. (2002). A knowledge base for the teaching profession: What would it look like and how can we get one? *Educational Research, 31*(5), 3–15.

Hill, C. J., Bloom, H. S., Black, A. R., & Lypsey, M. W. (2007). Empirical benchmarks for interpreting effect sizes in research. *Child Development Perspectives, 2*(3), 172–177.

Holloway, D. L. (2002). Using research to ensure quality teaching in rural schools. *Journal of Research in Rural Education, 17*(3), 138–153.

Howley, A., & Howley, C. B. (2005). High quality teaching: Providing for rural teachers professional development. *The Rural Educator, 26*(2), 12–16.

Hudson, P., Miller, S., Salzberg, C., & Morgan, R. (1994). The role of peer coaching in teacher education programs. *Teacher Education and Special Education, 17*(4), 224–235.

Hughes, M. F. (1999). Similar students—dissimilar opportunities for success: High- and low-achieving elementary schools in rural, high poverty areas of West Virginia. *Journal of Research in Rural Education, 15*(1), 47–58.

Ingersoll, R., & Smith, T. (2003). The wrong solution to the teacher shortage. *Educational Leadership, 60*(8) 30–33.

Institute of Educational Sciences. (n.d.). Teacher Professional Development in 1999–2000. Available at http://nces.ed.gov/pubs2006/2006305.pdf.

Jarzabkowski, L. (2003). Teacher collegiality in a remote Australian school. *Journal of Research in Rural Education, 18*(3), 139–144.

Kane, T. J. (2004). *The impact of after-school programs: Interpreting the results of four recent evaluations* [White Paper]. Available at http://www.sp2.upenn.edu/ostrc/doclibrary/documents/TheImpactofAfterSchoolProgramsthatPromotePersonalandSocialSkills_000.pdf.

Kaufman, R. C., & Wandberg, R. W. (2010). *Powerful practices for high-performing special educators.* Thousand Oaks, CA: Corwin Press.

Kenny, D. (2010). A teacher quality manifesto. Available at http://online.wsj.com/article/SB10001424052748703440604575496281030445268.html.

Kohm, B. (2002). Opening schools for discussion. *Educational Leadership, 59*(8), 31–33.

Knowles, M. (1980). *The modern practice of adult education: From pedagogy to andragogy.* New York, NY: Cambridge University Press.

Knowles, M. (1984). *Andragogy in action: Applying modern principles of adult learning.* San Francisco, CA: Jossey-Bass.

Kreitner, R., & Kinicki, A. (2012). *Organizational behavior* (10th edn.). New York, NY: McGraw-Hill/Irwin.

Lambert, L. (2002). A framework for shared leadership. *Educational Leadership, 59*(8), 37–40. Available at http://www.ascd.org/publications/educational-leadership/may02/vol59/num08/A-Framework-for-Shared-Leadership.aspx.

Lemlech, J. K. (1995). *Becoming a professional leader.* New York, NY: Scholastic.

Lieberman, A. (1995). Practices that support teacher development. *Phi Delta Kappa, 76,* 591–596.

Loucks-Horsely, S., Hewson, P. W., Love, N., & Stiles, K. E. (1998). *Designing professional development for teachers of science and mathematics.* Thousand Oaks, CA: Corwin Press.

Loughran, J. (1997). Understanding self-study of teacher education practices. In J. Loughran & T. Russell (Eds.), *Improving teacher education practices through self-study* (pp. 239–248). London: RoutledgeFalmer.

Loughran, J. (2002). Effective reflective practice in search of meaning in learning about teaching. *Journal of Teacher Education, 53*(1), 33–43.

McLaughlin, M., & Overturf, B. J. (2013). The common core: insights into the K–5 standards. *The Reading Teacher 66*(2): 1536–164.

Martin, G. A., & Double, J. M. (1998). Developing higher education teaching skills through peer observation and collaborative reflection. *Innovations in Education and Training International, 35*(2), 161–170.

Massachusetts Institute of Technology (MIT) Human Resources Department (2012). Giving effective feedback: a 4-part model. http://hrweb.mit.edu/performance-development/ongoing-feedback/giving-effective-feedback.

Mento, A. J., & Giampetro-Meyer, A. (2000). Peer observation of teaching as a true developmental opportunity. *College Teaching, 48*(1), 28–31.

MetLife. (2013). *Implementing the Common Core States Standards* [Issue Brief]. Available at http://www.achieve.org/files/RevisedElementaryAction Brief_Final_Feb.pdf.

Park, S., Oliver, J. S., Johnson, T. S., Graham, P., & Oppong, N. K. (2007). Colleagues' roles in the professional development of teachers: Results from a research study of National Board Certification. *Teaching & Teacher Education, 23*(4), 368–389.

Peel, D. (2005). Peer observation as a transformatory tool? *Teaching in Higher Education, 10*(4), 489–504.

Peterson, A. (2013). Biggest shift of Common Core is not the "what" we are teaching but "how", says E4E-NY teacher Amber Peterson. Available at http://www.educators4excellence.org/news/2013-12-biggest-shift-of-common-core-is-not-what-we-are-teach.

Phillips, V., & Hughes, R. (2012). Teacher collaboration: The essential Common Core ingredient. *Education Weekly*. Available at http://www.edweek.org/ew/articles/2012/12/05/13hughes.h32.html.

Pink, D. (2009). *Drive: The surprising truth about what motivates us.* New York, NY: Riverhead Books.

Pressick-Kilborn, K., & Riele, K. (2008). Learning from reciprocal peer observation: A collaborative self-study. *Studying Teacher Education, 4*(1), 61–75.

Rabin, R. (2013). *Blended learning for leadership: The CCL approach* [White Paper]. Available at http://www.ccl.org/leadership/pdf/research/BlendedLearningLeadership.pdf.

Ragland, K. M. (2005). *Teachers' attitudes regarding the collaborative elements involved in the inclusion of atypical learners in the general education classroom* (doctoral dissertation). Available from Dissertation Abstracts International (UMI No. 3184475).

Reed, P. (2013). Leadership skills for implementing the Common Core. *Principal Leadership.* Available at www.nassp.org/Content/158/pl_feb13_brip.pdf.

Reeves, D. B. (2009). *Leading change in your school.* Alexandria, VA: ASCD.

Reeves, D. B. (2010). *Transforming professional development into student results.* Alexandria, VA: ASCD.

Richards, J., & Farrell, T. (2005). *Professional development for language teachers: Strategies for teacher learning.* Cambridge, MA: Cambridge University Press.

Schmoker, M. (1999). *Results: The key to continuous school improvement* (2nd ed.). Alexandria, VA: Association for Supervision and Curriculum Development.

Schuck, S., Aubusson, P., & Buchanan, J. (2008). Enhancing teacher educational practice through professional learning conversations. *European Journal of Teacher Education, 31*(2), 215–227.

Shields, P. M., Marsh, J. A., & Adelman, N. E. (1998). *Evaluation of NSF's Statewide Systemic Initiatives (SSI) program: The SSI's impact on the classroom practice.* Menlo Park, CA: SRI.

Showers, B., & Joyce, B. (1996). The evolution of peer coaching. *Educational Leadership, 53*(6), 12–16.

Sparks, D. (2002). *Designing powerful professional development for teachers and principals.* Available at www.eric.ed.gov/ERICWebPortal/recordDetail?accno=ED470239.

Sparks, D., & Hirsh, S. (1997). *A new vision for staff development.* Alexandria, VA: ASCD.

Speck, M., & Knipe, C. (2005). *Why can't we get it right? Designing high-quality professional development for standards-based schools* (2nd edn.). Thousand Oaks, CA: Corwin Press.

Sprenger, M. (2013). 11 tips on teaching the common Core critical vocabulary. *Edutopia.* Available at www.edutopia.org/blog/teaching-ccss-critical-vocabulary-marilee-sprenger.

Stephenson, R. (n.d.) Increasing rigor through questioning strategies. Available at www.nassp.org/Content.aspx?topic=57408.

Straughter, B. (2001). *The effects of peer observation on self-governance among elementary teachers.* Unpublished doctoral dissertation. Argosy University.

Strucchelli, A. (2009). *Inquiry in the classroom: Peer observation as a form of job-embedded professional learning.* Unpublished doctoral dissertation. Argosy University.

United States (U.S.) Department of Commerce. (2010). *2010 Census urban and rural classification and urban area criteria.* Available at http://www.census.gov/geo/www/ua/2010urbanruralclass.html.

United States (U.S.) Department of Education. (2010). *A blueprint for reform: The reauthorization of the Elementary and Secondary Education Act.* Available at http://www2.ed.gov/policy/elsec/leg/blueprint/blueprint.pdf.

Vacilotto, S., & Cummings, R. (2007). Peer coaching in TEFL/TESL programmes. *ELT Journal, 61*(2), 153–160.

Vygotsky, L. S. (1978). *Mind in society: The development of higher psychological processes.* Cambridge, MA: Harvard University Press.

Vygotsky, L. S. (1986). *Thought and language.* Cambridge, MA: MIT Press.

Wei, R. C., Darling-Hammond, L., & Adamson, F. (2010). *Professional development in the United States: Trends and challenges* [White Paper]. Dallas, TX: National Staff Development Council.

Wilkins, E. A., Shin, E., & Ainsworth, J. (2009). The effects of peer feedback practices with elementary education teacher candidates. *Teacher Education Quarterly, 36*(2), 79–93.

Williamson, R., & Blackburn, B. (n.d.). Recognizing rigor in classrooms: Four tools for school leaders. Available at http://www.principals.org/tabid/3788/ default.aspx?topic=Recognizing_Rigor_in_Classrooms_Four_Tools_for_ School_Leaders_.

Wilson, L. (2012). 5 things geese can teach us about teamwork. Available at http://lenwilson.us/5-thing-geese-can-teach-us-about-teamwork/.

Yoon, K. S., Duncan, T., Lee, S. W., Scarloss, B., & Shapley, K. L. (2007). *Reviewing the evidence on how teacher professional development affects student achievement* [Policy Brief]. Available at the Regional Education Laboratory: http://www.ies.ed.gov/ncee/edlabs/regions/southwest/pdf/rel_ 2007033.pdf.

Zwart, R. C., Wubbels, T., Bergen, T. C., & Bolhuis, S. (2007). Experienced teacher learning within the context of reciprocal peer coaching. *Teachers and Teaching: Theory and practice, 13*(2), 165–187.

Appendices

Peer Observation, Feedback, and Reflection

Teacher: _____   Subject: _____ Period: _____

Observer: _____ Date: _____

Instruction

Questions/Wonderings/Suggestions

_____

_____

Engagement (structured participation)

_____ students actively paraphrasing their partner's/other student's response, building on ideas, etc.

_____ sentence frames etc. supporting complete sentences and use of academic language, structured written responses

_____ power sentences (structured use of academic language/critical thinking), structured individual responses

_____ circulating as students working (giving feedback)

_____ students working together giving each other constructive feedback (peer revising . . .)

Academic rigor (critical thinking/academic language/vocabulary)

_____ appropriate range/level of prompts (Bloom's taxonomy)

_____ students regularly explain thinking, explain answers, justify with logic/evidence

_____ teacher clearly modeling thinking—think aloud, explaining . . .

____ students taught/prompted to ask/answer questions at various levels
____ students taught to self-evaluate understanding (*metacognition*)

Evidence of planning (utilizing UBD/data analysis)
____ direct link between daily lesson and final assessment
____ students aware of what they are doing and how it fits into current unit of study
____ teacher can explain where he/she is in current unit (will be based on discussion either before or after the observation)
____ "next steps" in place—how do we know if students are getting it? What are we doing if they're not?

We can use this last section as a starting point for our conversations.

Peer Observation Checklist
Gradual Release of Responsibility Instructional Model
Teacher being observed _____
Date _____

1. "I do."
   Objective was both written on the board and verbalized   _____
   Prior knowledge was determined   _____
   Relevancy was given for the specific objective   _____
   Needed vocabulary was taught   _____
   Success criteria was established   _____
   Skill was modeled by teacher   _____
Notes _____
   _____
   _____

2. "We do."
   Students are directed to work along with the teacher   _____
   Teacher moves around the room checking for understanding   _____
   Students might work in pairs   _____
   Multiple opportunities are given for practice   _____
Notes _____
   _____
   _____

3. "You do."
   Students are given opportunities to try on their own   _____
   Success criteria are measured   _____

Notes _____

    _____

    _____

I noticed
that _____

_____

_____

I wonder
about _____

_____

_____

Peer Observation Checklist

Teacher: _____   Subject: _____

Observer: _____   Duration: _____

☐ Entire Class Time: Initial Observation		DATE:	
☐ Part Class Time: Targeted observation		*2 Month Cycle	
Month	Date	Month	Date
September		February	
October		March	
November		April	
December		May	
January			

Routine Events that are observed: What is the teacher doing to _____

Establish and Communicate Learning Goals	Track Student Progress and Check for Student Understanding	Establish or Maintain Classroom Expectations and Procedures
Things to look for ELTs Lesson opener	*Things to look for* Questioning Re-teaching Specific Corrective Feedback	*Things to look for* Smooth and timely transitions Time on task Student behaviors Routines and procedures Expectations Consistency

Content: What is the teacher doing to _____

Help Students Effectively Interact with New Knowledge (Delivery)	Help Students Practice and/or Apply Knowledge (Guided Practice)	
Things to look for Modeling of skills Vocabulary Making connections Building background Active thinking Signaling	*Things to look for* Corrective feedback Re-teaching Differentiation	*Activities* How are the students practicing? How involved are the students with the learning?

Peer Observation Attitudinal Survey
Created by Dr. Kristen(Kaye) Ragland
Modified by Dr. CherylAnn Bourne-Hayes

1. Peer Observation is the best form of professional development for all teachers.

   Strongly disagree ☐
   Disagree ☐
   Undecided ☐
   Agree ☐

2. Novice teachers are well served through Peer Observation.

   Strongly disagree ☐
   Disagree ☐
   Undecided ☐
   Agree ☐

3. Veteran teachers are well served through Peer Observation.

   Strongly disagree ☐
   Disagree ☐
   Undecided ☐
   Agree ☐

4. Peer Observation will improve teaching skills.

   Strongly disagree ☐
   Disagree ☐
   Undecided ☐
   Agree ☐

5. Teachers are better served through other forms of professional development other than Peer Observation.

   Strongly disagree ☐
   Disagree ☐
   Undecided ☐
   Agree ☐

6. Many teachers are well served through Peer Observation with support.

Strongly disagree ☐
Disagree ☐
Undecided ☐
Agree ☐

7. Peer Observation is a beneficial form of ongoing professional development.

Strongly disagree ☐
Disagree ☐
Undecided ☐
Agree ☐

8. Collaboration in the Peer Observation process is necessary for professional growth.

Strongly disagree ☐
Disagree ☐
Undecided ☐
Agree ☐

9. All members of the Peer Observation team, including veteran and novice teachers, should share equal responsibility for professional growth.

Strongly disagree ☐
Disagree ☐
Undecided ☐
Agree ☐

10. Peer Observation administrative responsibilities, such as devising an observation checklist, should be equally shared between all teachers involved in the process.

Strongly disagree ☐
Disagree ☐
Undecided ☐
Agree ☐

11. A novice teacher should hold primary responsibility for the planning of the Peer Observation process with support from the other teachers involved.

Strongly disagree ☐
Disagree ☐
Undecided ☐
Agree ☐

12. It is important that the unique gifts, talents, knowledge, and expertise of each member of a Peer Observation team be acknowledged and valued.

Strongly disagree ☐
Disagree ☐
Undecided ☐
Agree ☐

13. Peer Observation team members should share the same educational philosophy.

Strongly disagree ☐
Disagree ☐
Undecided ☐
Agree ☐

14. Peer Observation team members should utilize the same methodologies and techniques.

Strongly disagree ☐
Disagree ☐
Undecided ☐
Agree ☐

15. Teachers should be involved in the selection of those with whom they will participate in a Peer Observation team.

Strongly disagree ☐
Disagree ☐
Undecided ☐
Agree ☐

16. Clear open communication between Peer Observation team members is imperative for successful collaboration.

Strongly disagree ☐
Disagree ☐
Undecided ☐
Agree ☐

17. Clear expectations are imperative for successful collaboration in the Peer Observation process.

Strongly disagree ☐
Disagree ☐
Undecided ☐
Agree ☐

18. Scheduled shared planning time is imperative for successful collaboration.

Strongly disagree ☐
Disagree ☐
Undecided ☐
Agree ☐

19. Strong administrative support is a requirement for successful collaboration.

Strongly disagree ☐
Disagree ☐
Undecided ☐
Agree ☐

20. Most veteran teachers are knowledgeable enough about their needs to collaborate successfully in Peer Observation.

Strongly disagree ☐
Disagree ☐
Undecided ☐
Agree ☐

21. Most novice teachers are knowledgeable enough about their needs to collaborate successfully in Peer Observation.

    Strongly disagree ☐
    Disagree ☐
    Undecided ☐
    Agree ☐

22. Teacher education departments (universities) should prepare all students for the Peer Observation process.

    Strongly disagree ☐
    Disagree ☐
    Undecided ☐
    Agree ☐

23. In order to successfully collaborate in the Peer Observation process, members of the Peer Observation must be committed to the concept of Peer Observation.

    Strongly disagree ☐
    Disagree ☐
    Undecided ☐
    Agree ☐

24. I am knowledgeable enough about Peer Observation to participate comfortably in implementing it.

    Strongly disagree ☐
    Disagree ☐
    Undecided ☐
    Agree ☐

25. Inservice training in the Peer Observation process would increase my comfort level with participating.

    Strongly disagree ☐
    Disagree ☐
    Undecided ☐
    Agree ☐

26. Stronger administrative support would increase my comfort level with participating in Peer Observation.

Strongly disagree ☐
Disagree ☐
Undecided ☐
Agree ☐

27. A school culture of open communication would increase my comfort level with participating in Peer Observation.

Strongly disagree ☐
Disagree ☐
Undecided ☐
Agree ☐

28. A school culture of shared leadership for professional development would increase my comfort level with working with teams for Peer Observation.

Strongly disagree ☐
Disagree ☐
Undecided ☐
Agree ☐

29. It is hard to imagine having a colleague observe me in my classroom.

Strongly disagree ☐
Disagree ☐
Undecided ☐
Agree ☐

30. I prefer the independence of the traditional classroom, and would rather not engage in Peer Observation.

Strongly disagree ☐
Disagree ☐
Undecided ☐
Agree ☐

31. I can embrace the changes in the collegial relationships with my professional peers that are a result of the Peer Observation process.

Strongly disagree ☐
Disagree ☐
Undecided ☐
Agree ☐

32. I am comfortable with the concept of Peer Observation and support it as an effective means of professional development.

Strongly disagree ☐
Disagree ☐
Undecided ☐
Agree ☐